GOD IS NOT THROUGH WITH ME YET

THELMA WELLS

Multnomah Publishers

THIS WORK IS DEDICATED to God Almighty, who is the Person I write about. He is the Author and Finisher of my faith, my joy, my peace, my all. Without Him, I would not have a story of triumph to talk about. You are my Mighty God. • Jesus, without Your saving power to rescue a person as sinful as I, and the price You paid on the cross, I would still be condemned to eternal death. But You chose to rescue me from the depths of sin and sickness. I appreciate You. • Thanks, Holy Spirit, for dictating this book to me through my experiences and the study of the Word of God, the Bible. As You spoke in my spirit, I wrote. It would have been impossible for me to have written these words without Your prompting. • To the you who read this book, I dedicate the words to your heart and soul that you may become stronger in your mortal body, your inquiring soul, and your God-given spirit to caress the beauty of the Holiness and God who is the great I AM — because God is not through with YOU yet!

GOD IS NOT THROUGH WITH ME YET
published by Multnomah Publishers
A division of Random House Inc.
Published in association with Van Diest Literary Agency

International Standard Book Number: 1-59052-785-2
Cover photo by Marquette, Simple Treasures Photography

Italics in Scripture quotes are the author's emphasis.

Printed in the United States of America

For information:
MULTNOMAH PUBLISHERS
12265 Oracle Boulevard, Suite 200
Colorado Springs, Colorado 80921

LIBRARY OF CONGRESS CATALOGING-IN-PUBLICATION DATA
Wells, Thelma, 1941-
God is not through with me yet / Thelma Wells.
p. cm.
ISBN 1-59052-785-2
1. Christian life. 2. Jesus Christ--Person and offices. I. Title.
BV4501.3.W423 2007
248.4--dc22

2006031277

07 08 09 10 11 12—10 9 8 7 6 5 4 3 2 1 0

Contents

Introduction: Success Comes in Cans 4

Part I: I Can...

1. He Keeps Me Singing 13
2. Experience Is an Able Teacher 31
3. He Prepares, and He Provides 41
4. A Path to Humility 58
5. Learning to Pray 71

Part II: ...Because I Know the I AM

6. The Great I AM 91
7. I AM Is Your Healer 101
8. I AM Is Your Provider 121
9. I AM Is Your Banner 137
10. The Power Connection 153
11. Obedience Really Is Better 163

Part III: For Your Reflection

12. Thoughts in the Morning 187

Special Section 1: Christ the I AM 197
Special Section 2: Secrets of Prayer 212
Special Section 3: Healing Scriptures 227
Acknowledgments 255

INTRODUCTION

SUCCESS COMES IN CANS

In a hotel suite in Somewhere, USA, I stepped into the living room area and was immediately captivated by a framed poster on the wall. It was a painting of a thirty-gallon metal trashcan set against a sky blue background. Gracefully emerging out of the trashcan was a beautiful iris blossom held up by a strong green stem and accented by two long, green leaves. And written on the trashcan's side were these words: "Success Comes in Cans."

The image stayed with me, in the forefront of my mind. For days and days I thought about the reality that success really does come in "cans"—that anything we put our minds to do, and want to do badly enough, we *can* do it.

I started teaching others that the word *can't* is misleading.

I explained how we tend to prioritize our cans. We can practice piano lessons when we want to, or find an excuse and say, "I can't." We can memorize anything we put our minds to, but if it seems hard, we quickly say, "I can't."

There really are some things that we cannot do—things that are simply too challenging for us physically, mentally, or emotionally. *But beside every "can't" there is a "can."*

I cannot become a star ballerina at my age; but if I had the desire (which I don't), I *could* take lessons, and have fun doing it. I cannot give away all the money I want to (and this is a true desire for me) because I don't have that kind of money; but I *can* give what I have, and be grateful I have it to give.

The True "I Can"

But that's not the complete story about our "cans."

Philippians 4:13 says, *"I can do all things through Christ who strengthens me."* This is really the perfect "Success Comes in Cans" situation. People often mistake this passage to mean that for everything we want to have or to do, if we just ask Jesus for it, then it becomes ours for the taking. No. I don't believe that. God has ordained each of us to do certain and specific things in life, and each of us is called to do them in our own way, because we're uniquely put together by God. The fact is, the "all things" in this verse means *all things that God has assigned us to do*, with the help of Jesus Christ living in our lives and being our Lord and Master. That's what this verse is assuring us that we *can* do.

And when we do what God has made us to do, we are strengthened for it in our body, soul, and spirit. Therefore I can speak because God called and equipped me to speak. I can write because God assigned me to write. I can sing because God gave me a voice to sing. I can nurture people because God instilled within me a mothering, nurturing heart. I can love because God placed His Spirit of love inside me when I asked His Son to come into my heart.

So…I *can* do all things that God made me to do, that God tells me to do, that God enables me to do—because I know Him as God, I've accepted His Son as my Savior, and I have His Holy Spirit living inside my heart.

Consequently, *I can*…because I know the I AM—God's revealed name for Himself, which we'll explore in-depth in these pages.

In this book, I talk about how to know *I can* because *I know the I AM.* I see this book as an eye-opener to the blindness of our arrogant "I can!" thinking that has forgotten all about God.

Wrapped Up in "I Am"

How many times a day do you use the phrase "I am"?

"I am hungry…"

"I am tired…"

"I am busy…"

"I am hurting…"

The "I am's" can go on and on.

Listen to a newborn baby's cry. That baby's saying, "I am in need of something." And watch how we keep it up as we grow older and more mature. We never stop saying, "I am in need of something."

There's not a person anywhere who hasn't wrapped themselves around those two little words *I am.* And have you thought about the fact that the first word in all our "I am's" is "I"? We all enjoy talking about ourselves more than anybody else. For each of us, our inner radio is tuned to station WIIFM (What's In It For Me?).

When I feel I'm in control, I totally deceive myself to make myself feel important. But who can count on feelings?

One big part of that is how we all want to be in control of ourselves and of our loved ones. We want to think we can make our own decisions, create our own career paths, handle our own circumstances, and solve our own problems without someone else's aid. We think that way—until our backs are up against the wall and we're between a rock and a hard place. That's when we submit, for the moment at least, to God—who is higher than our thoughts and greater than our power to control.

Over the past sixty-plus years, I have discovered and even submitted to the fact that I'm not in control of *anything.* When I *feel* I'm in control, I totally deceive myself to make myself feel important. But who can count on feelings?

I now know that in the stuff of life, the only way I can get the best results is through knowing the Great I AM....

Trust the Great I AM

It's so true that I am needy. I have endless needs! I get hungry and need to be fed. I get weary and need rest. I get hurt and need help. I get sick and need healing. I get confused and need guidance. I get scared and need protection. I get bogged down in life and need deliverance. I lose track of who I am and need a reminder. And goodness, I have a lot more needs—and I know I need the Great I AM.

I have learned more deeply than ever to feel God's presence...because I know the I AM is always with me.

Someone asks me, "Have you ever felt like you were far away from God, even though you've accepted Him as your Lord?"

My answer: Sure, Sweetie. Early in my adulthood I often thought I was far from God and that He was far from me. There were times when I couldn't see or feel Him. In the back of my mind I *thought* He was there, but we just didn't seem to be communicating about anything.

So many believers are walking around with the same feelings of distance from God. So many are walking around defeated. They have tried all the programs, they have read all the how-to books, they have followed the seven keys to a successful...(you name it)—but they've come up short, again and again. They're tired and ready to give up. Why is it this way?

Because they haven't given in to the I AM. They're still trying to go it on their own and bring in God only when the rough times come.

To be able to see our lives and ourselves clearly—so we can do great feats, overcome limitations, deal with hurt and disappointment, forgive from the heart, and successfully tackle all the other stuff of life—there is only *one means*. And that is to trust and follow the Great I AM.

If we all were honest with ourselves, we would know we can't live up to the "standard." We don't have what it takes. We fall far short of our desired goals. And sometimes, when we're *really* honest, we recognize that we're just plain tired of being *us*—the excuses we make for our shortcomings, the lies and half-lies we tell to make us sound better than we are.

The neat thing is, all you have to do is *give up*.

The fact is, we're all a mess. But if we could just let go—die to ourselves—then and only then can God take over and truly live through us.

The Bible says, "Humble yourselves under the mighty hand of God, that He may exalt you in due time" (1 Peter 5:6). But we have to die to our own agendas and our own plans and realize how needy and sinful we really are.

Success…or Sinner?

There was a time when I thought, *I can*—all on my own. And I had some success at it.

But the Lord has been gracious enough to bless me with significant trials—trials that have brought me low, and I've seen Him lift me higher than I have ever known.

I see myself like the woman washing Jesus' feet in the Pharisee's house—"she is a sinner" (Luke 7:39). She brought herself low, but Jesus lifted her up. Despite her many sins, He lifted her up because of her humility and total brokenness. I want to help people to be "brought low" so that Christ, in His infinite mercy, can lift them up.

PART I

I CAN...

CHAPTER 1

HE KEEPS ME SINGING

In the 1920s and '30s, a certain little girl was growing up with severe physical deformities that would mark her for life.

Her whole right side was paralyzed. She could not extend her right arm, which had a permanent bend, and the fingers on her right hand looked like long chicken's feet matted together. Her right leg was twisted, and her deformed right foot turned inward. Even her lips were a little twisted on one side.

As this little girl was growing up, her mother was so angry about her child's condition that she would often attempt to straighten out the deformed hand and foot by vigorously turning and twisting them, but without success. When those efforts didn't work, her mother would beat her and put her in a closet out of her sight.

The little girl's father was more compassionate and understanding. He loved his daughter. All her life he tried to teach her the ways of God, to shelter her from harm, to comfort her when people made fun of her, to hold her when she was sad, to encourage her in her school work, and to sweetly discipline her when she needed it.

One day, after their deformed daughter had grown into a teenager, the parents were devastated and appalled to learn that she was pregnant.

It was too much for the girl's mother to take. She said she was already taking care of a crippled daughter, and she was not about to take care of her baby too. The girl's father, however, wanted her to stay in the safety of their home after the baby came, in spite of the embarrassment and sadness of this situation. But the mother was insistent: Her daughter and the baby would have to get out of her house and make it on their own.

So when the child was born—a little girl—this unwed teenage mother found work as a maid cleaning "the big house" while living with her baby daughter in servants' quarters. She toiled away with her one good hand and foot.

A Surprising Change

Two years later, both she and her baby became critically ill. Her mother was contacted and asked to nurse the baby back to health, but she still refused to bring her daughter's baby into her home.

The young woman's father, however, contacted his own sixty-year-old mother to ask if she would care for the sick baby. He promised to provide financial help and to do all he could to assist her with this child.

This woman, who was a true woman of God, eagerly accepted this responsibility of caring for her great-granddaughter. With all the love in her heart, she was determined that this child should live.

So the little girl was brought to her and her husband, and the crippled young mother was told that her baby would be returned to her when they both were well.

By the time the baby recovered, the two great-grandparents had become deeply attached to this child, and it was hard for them to imagine giving her up. But they had made a covenant with the mother to return the baby to her—and they were people of their word, no matter how difficult it was to part from their little great-granddaughter.

They called the young mother to say that her daughter was well enough to go home. To their delight and surprise, the young mother told them she thought the baby would have a better life living with them than with her. She made it clear, however, that she was not abandoning the child; the young mother was adamant that she needed a relationship with her daughter and wanted to be able to see her whenever she wanted.

The great-grandparents quickly agreed. This covenant, too, was one that they kept, for as the girl grew up in their home she was allowed to have an open and loving relationship with her mother, and the mother was never denied access to her.

This young child's life was wonderful with her great-grandparents. They loved God with every fiber of their being, and they led the little girl to Christ—she gave her heart to the Lord as a four-year-old. They took her to church all the time, where she especially learned to love the hymns that were sung there.

Sometimes the girl and her great-grandfather would play "Prayer Meeting." They would pray long "prayers," and "read Scriptures," and sing, sing, sing. One of the great-grandfather's favorite songs was this one:

I shall not, I shall not be moved;
I shall not, I shall not be moved;
just like a tree that's planted by the water,
I shall not be moved.

The little girl kept this in her memory.

A Dark Closet

There were occasions when the girl was taken to her mother's parents to stay for a while at their house. On these visits, her granddaddy loved her, played with her, took her to movies and the park, gave her rides on the train, and even took her shopping.

But it was much different with the grandmother, the woman who earlier had refused to let this child live with her when she was a baby. After the grandfather went to work, the grandmother would shut this little girl up in a dark, smelly, insect-infested closet to sit out the rest of the day, with no food or water or conversation. Just before time for the girl's granddaddy to return home from work, her grandmother would bring her out from the closet, clean her up, and act like all was well.

She would sing herself to sleep in the closet; and when she came out of the closet, she was not angry, bitter, hurt, or damaged in any way. What a miracle!

The little girl did not know why she was put in that closet; her grandmother told her it was to keep the iron from falling on her (likely story). But the little girl had been taught to obey adults, so she went into the closet upon demand.

She was scared in that closet. She had nothing to do in that closet. All she knew to do was to sing, because of what she had learned in church and from playing "Prayer

Meeting" with her great-grandfather. Sometimes she had to make up words when she couldn't quite remember them all, but she did her best to sing the songs of the church, like "Throw Out the Life Line," "Nearer My God to Thee," "Rock of Ages," "What a Friend We Have in Jesus," "The Old Rugged Cross," "Amazing Grace," and "Jesus Loves Me, This I Know."

She would sing herself to sleep in the closet; and when she came out of the closet, she was not angry, bitter, hurt, or damaged in any way. What a miracle! The Lord had received this little girl's innocent praise and had rewarded it with a little abundant life of joy.

In time, this little girl grew up to be an upstanding citizen in her community. Although many said that she would "never make it," she became a trailblazer for other black women, a prominent international speaker and author, and a wife, mother, grandmother, and great-grandmother herself.

It took many years before this girl understood the significance of singing in that closet at her grandmother's house. It was not until she was grown up and married and had two children, and was verging on a nervous breakdown, that she remembered in the clearest way the peace and tranquility of singing in the closet. She realized she had experienced calmness by singing church songs that quieted her down when she wanted to go on a rage.

So now, in her adulthood, the memory of the closet helped her realize that when she wanted to cry, she could instead resort to singing or humming or listening to a Christian music album. She learned to do this as well when she held her babies or nursed her ailing, aging, great-grandmother. Each time the music would play, negative attitudes would subside, and she would find herself in a more soothing spirit. Listening to inspirational and gospel music became a habit for her, a ritual in her home. And not only did it soothe her, but it would also calm her kids and lull to sleep her great-grandmother.

Discovering the therapeutic power of Christian music was not an instant revelation for her, but one that evolved over years of applying it during periods of hurt, disappointment, neglect, questionable hope, anger, disillusionment, lack of harmony, unkind deeds, financial difficulties, seemingly unanswered prayers, and disbelief. In this way, these moments would become a time of spiritual growth.

Unanswered Questions

Are you wondering who this person is, who had such an unpromising start in life as the child of a cast-out, unwed teenage mother?

I'll tell you.

The only name on that baby girl's birth certificate was "Baby Girl Morris" (a fact that she didn't discover until decades later, after considerable investigation). But the name she grew up with (and which was listed on her baptism and school records) was Thelma Louise Smith—until she married at age twenty and became Thelma Wells.

Yes, it's me!

That last name of "Morris" was apparently the attempt of my mysterious father, or somebody, to cover up my mother's sin. When I started, as an adult, to seek more answers about my birth, my childhood, and my father, nobody was willing to discuss this situation. My mother had the answers, but each time I asked her she would say, "You don't need to know about that," or "I'm not talking to you about that." I was mature enough to understand even the worst situation, but I was denied access to my history and background. It all went to the graves of my mother, father, and grandparents.

And so the now aging child of this crippled, unwed teenager still wonders sometimes what the real deal was. I'll never know, until I get to glory. So I've rested my case. To all my still unanswered questions, I just apply the Word of God: "The secret things belong to the LORD our God, but those things which are revealed belong to us and to our children forever" (Deuteronomy 29:29).

But one thing from my childhood that is *not* an unanswered secret is the discovery I made in that nasty closet of the worth of praise and worship. I didn't fully realize its true value for years; but I did know that *He kept me singing.*

I would think of him, and sing those hymns—and I realized *I had a friend in Jesus,* a wonderful friend. And I would sing (making up the words where necessary) something like this:

> *What a Friend we have in Jesus, all our sins and*
> *griefs to bear!*
> *What a privilege to carry everything to God*
> *in prayer!*
> *O what peace we often forfeit, O what needless*
> *pain we bear,*
> *All because we do not carry everything to God*
> *in prayer.*
> *Have we trials and temptations? Is there trouble*
> *anywhere?*
> *We should never be discouraged; take it to the Lord*
> *in prayer.*
> *Can we find a friend so faithful who will all our*
> *sorrows share?*
> *Jesus knows our every weakness; take it to the Lord*
> *in prayer.*

Though I was only a little girl, and though I had to make up some of the words to the song, I knew I could take my situation to Jesus, because Jesus is indeed my Friend. I knew that if I would call on Him, whether I had the words right or not, He would be right there. And praise be to God, I walked out of that closet on those days having no bitterness, no anger, no animosity, nothing, because God met me at the point of my need.

And He will meet *you* at the point of your need, because *you* have—oh, glory!—a friend in Jesus.

Singing in the Closets of Life

In all the closets of my life, I have learned to sing. When my body is racked with pain, I sing. When my budget is in excess of my income, I sing. When my relationships take a turn for the worse, I sing. When I don't understand what's going on in the government, I sing. When my children need assistance, I sing. When church feels uninviting, I sing. When I've missed an important engagement or assignment, I sing. When I don't feel like doing my housework, I sing. When things don't go my way, I sing. When storms come and the electricity is off, I sing. When the scales don't show me losing weight, I sing.

Yes, *He* keeps me singing! There's not a circumstance in my life that I don't sing my way through, just like an old hymn says:

There's within my heart a melody
Jesus whispers sweet and low:
"Fear not, I am with thee; peace, be still,"
in all of life's ebb and flow.
Jesus, Jesus, Jesus,
sweetest name I know,
fills my every longing,
keeps me singing as I go.

Life is full of ups and downs, uncertainties, issues, and situations. But in every one of them, God gives me peaceful consolation that when I sing praises to Him, He hears me and rejoices over me.

A Universal Language

Music is one of our love letters to God, and also His love response back to me. Christian praise music is the exterminator of the enemy of our souls. When we sing praises or keep praise music playing in our houses, cars, workplaces, or anywhere else, the atmosphere changes for the better. It is my firm belief that praise music chases away any foul spirits that are in our midst. The Lord inhabits our praises, and when praise is going on, Satan cannot stand to be in the same place where the Lord of Hosts dwells.

Christian music can calm a crying baby, ease a broken heart, soothe a troubled mind, open a closed mind, relieve a wounded spirit, comfort a grieving soul, speak peace to a sick body, disarm a combative person, defuse an angry person, captivate a longing desire, break down the walls of prejudice and injustice, set the atmosphere for worship, and speak messages of hope and encouragement to all of our hearts.

Singing will help your worries and anguish fade away like bubbles that succumb to still water. Singing will make you wonder why you were so mad. Singing can turn your adversary into your friend.

I didn't know how important music was in my life until I had hardships and regrets. But I learned to praise my way out of every situation. Some situations last for years and years, but if you can sing, hum, play music, or listen to it, your world will be an easier place to face your problems and work out your dilemmas.

Music is indeed a universal language. The tunes and often the words of great church music are recognized all over the world. I've visited many foreign countries, and everywhere I've gone, I've heard people singing (often in their native tongue) "Amazing Grace" as well as other hymns that are old and familiar to me.

I visited a village in South Africa several years ago, together with the ladies I speak with at the Women of Faith conferences. In one South African setting we participated in the mourning tradition of sitting with the bereaved and singing and praying with them. When we began to sing the hymn "It Is Well with My Soul," each of the mourners joined in, singing either in English or Zulu. It was a stirring moment of harmony, comfort, and even joy at the blending of nations in one accord with music.

Praise Moves Heaven

I've learned in my sixty-five plus years that music is not only a universal language, it is also heavenly language understood by the God who made and ordered praise, the God who deserves all our praise, the God who is moved by our praise.

The Lord Himself sings along in our music.

One of the most powerful praise stories is found in the book of Acts when Paul and Silas were in jail:

> But at midnight Paul and Silas were praying and singing hymns to God, and the prisoners were listening to them. Suddenly there was a great earthquake, so that the foundations of the prison were shaken; and immediately all the doors were opened and everyone's chains were loosed. (Acts 16:25–26)

Now that's some powerful praise, baby!

Any time you're serious about your praise to God, and you buckle down and give it all you've got from a sincere and pure heart, you can shake up heaven, and God will move for you.

It's fascinating to study about praise music throughout the Bible. We find that musical praise of God has been going on since the universe began: Angels sang praise to God before the stars were put in space and before the earth was made.

We find also that music is not only a universal language, but also an eternal language. Those of us who are saved by grace through faith in Jesus Christ will forever sing praises to God in the New Jerusalem. We will join with the angels singing "Holy, holy, holy is the Lord God Almighty!"

According to Revelation 15:3, at the end of time the saints will be singing a song of victors:

> They sing the song of Moses, the servant of God, and the song of the Lamb, saying:
> *"Great and marvelous are Your works,*
> *Lord God Almighty!*
> *Just and true are Your ways,*
> *O King of the saints!*
> *Who shall not fear You, O Lord, and glorify*
> *Your name?*

For You alone are holy.
For all nations shall come and worship before You."
(vv. 3–4)

So to praise God with singing is entirely biblical. Praise and music are found hundreds of times in the Scriptures, throughout every part of God's Word. Praise is very important to God! Something happens in the heavenlies when we sing His praises, and that's why the Bible commands it:

Sing praises to God, sing praises!
Sing praises to our King, sing praises! (Psalm 47:6)

With music comes dancing, and to worship God in dance is a biblical command as well: "Praise Him with the timbrel and dance" (Psalm 150:4). Scripture gives many references to the use of dance as a form of joyous celebration and of reverent worship.

So check out the Book of the Psalms and be overcome by the praise of David and others as they "give it up" in praise to God. The psalmists hold nothing back; they just let it all out.

And the Lord Himself sings along in this music, just as He tells us: "The LORD your God in your midst…He will rejoice over you with singing" (Zephaniah 3:17). I love the way someone has portrayed this Scripture: The Daughters of Zion were dancing and singing in worship to the Lord God, and He asked them, "Is that a choir I hear?" Then He answered His own question: "No, that's Me rejoicing over them."

Imagine God rejoicing, walking on air, jubilant and dancing...*over us*! This blows my mind. It don't get no better than that! The Lord of lords and King of kings celebrating over you because you gave Him total praise!

Praise for His Glorious Grace

When my children were young and were perplexed, I would put music on for them. After they became adults, they have followed the same tradition of listening to music or singing. They're still lovers of inspirational music, and so are their spouses and children. In fact, my grandchildren are hams like their grandmother; they'll break out in song on a whim. They'll organize a "talent show" for the family dinners on Sundays, using a spoon or a flashlight as their microphone while they sing and dance like David danced to the Lord. The best thing about watching them is that they only know church music and praise dancing. Hallelujah!

I've always been quick to tell my family and friends how I feel when I listen to praise music. A few years ago, with their encouragement and help, I even recorded an album of praise and testimony.

I still remember the Saturday morning when my daughter Vikki scolded me and told me I had to start work on this album that very day. For several months we had been waiting to get started until my voice was clear from colds and bouts with a sore throat. But that morning, Vikki said the Lord told her it had to be done that day. Fortunately, the studio was in her cousin's home, and Vikki had called him to make sure it was available, as well as making arrangements with my accompanist.

So I prayed and told the Lord that this project was dedicated to Him. I asked Him to anoint me with the vocal ability and songs of praise that would edify people and glorify Him. Without any practice—just prayer and surrender—we went into the studio, and within two hours, our work was done. The album is called *His Glorious Grace: Testimony in Song*. (You can find out more about it in the back of this book.)

Ike Johnson, one of my preacher friends, told me that he cried the first time he listened to this music. Ike said that the entire album was so anointed that he wept in his car. He was soothed and so blessed that he wanted to share it with people who would not have access to it. Now he buys a lot of these albums from me to take to nursing homes and to the sick.

I'm So Glad

I'm so glad my great-grandmother took me to church seven days a week. I'm so glad my great-grandfather played "Prayer Meeting" with me. Otherwise I might not have learned the songs of the church and been able to sing them in that wretched closet as a little girl.

I'm so glad I remembered how soothed I was in the closet, and I came to understand and believe that the same soothing power of singing could continue to bring comfort when I was depressed and angry.

I'm so glad nobody has discouraged me from playing praise music and singing it.

I realize that I will have many more ups and downs in the days of my life. But I have an entrance to the Holy of Holies where I can meet God in praise, and He will rejoice over me with comfort and peace. He'll always keep me singing in the good times and in the bad. He is my High Musician who conducts the orchestra of my heartstrings with a symphony of His Glorious Praise.

He keeps me singing…because God is not through with me yet!

CHAPTER 2

EXPERIENCE IS AN ABLE TEACHER

I was pretty vexed at Reetie and Ruby. They were sick—and they wouldn't allow me to visit them.

It was such a puzzle, because we were very good friends. Reetie and I grew up together and had enjoyed five decades of close friendship; Ruby and I had traveled to foreign countries and roomed together without any confrontations.

So when these good friends faced chemo and radiation treatment, and I knew they were very sick, I phoned them several times—having already dressed to go see them, and ready to walk out the door. But the answer I got (either from them personally or from a caretaker) was always the same: No, they didn't want to see anybody today. I rerouted my day and made the best of it. But my feelings were hurt.

I prayed for them, inquired about them, and sent them get-well cards and flowers. But after all we'd been through together, they didn't even want to *see* me? What's up with that?

Eventually I discovered that everyone attempting to visit them was given the same answer, which made me feel a little better (you know how misery loves company). But I just couldn't comprehend their wish to have no visitors.

Then I faced my own critical illness...and learned an important and revealing lesson.

Out of It

After I had my first surgery in December of 2005, I was so out of it from the drugs and the recovery that I don't even remember some of my visitors in the hospital. It's all a fog. I think I recall seeing Ike and Gary, Francina and Lesa, and Ronnie and Shirley, but I can't tell you anything about their visits. They say I was cordial and delighted to see them (at least that's what they tell me; I surely don't know).

After going home, I remember Gwen, Derl, Shirley, Sharian, Carolyn, and others coming by, and I was glad to see them. I'd gotten lonesome for human contact that wasn't wearing a medical uniform.

Then I had a second surgery just a week and a half after the first. This time I was out like a light for several days. I was on life support in a special dormitory called the

Critical Intensive Care Unit, and, baby, I didn't know I was in this world. I could have gone on to see Jesus and woke up saying, *"Hey Jesus! I'm glad I'm home!"*

Even when they moved me to a private room, I slept more than I was awake. (Looking back, subconsciously I probably wanted to sleep through that liquid diet they had me on. Who wants colored water for dinner?)

As far as I can make out, I never said anything risqué—except, "And God can also cure booty rash."

When visitors came, I understand (from those who love me) that instead of them entertaining me, I entertained them. After the life support was taken away, they say I talked the whole while. They say I talked so much they kept asking me to be quiet so I could rest. I didn't even know I was tired; I was only doing what I do best—*talk.* (Don't they realize I'm a professional speaker? What's up with them?)

They say I told them to purchase some pretty white canvas bags from L. L. Bean. (I've never bought a thing from L. L. Bean. Where did that come from?)

They say I invited them to see a snow-white Christmas tree, the largest in the world, and to notice the huge pearl-white Christmas ornament in the center of it.

One lady who visited me says that I prayed for everybody in my family, for the world, and for people I didn't know (and people I probably didn't want to know).

Fortunately, as far I can make out, I never said anything risqué—except, "And God can also cure booty rash."

I understand that all ears were tuned in to hear me. (A word of caution: Put into your mind only what you're willing to release through your mouth—because if you're sedated or losing your mind, what's in you *will* come out.)

Hinged and Helpless

When I got home from this second surgery I was so weak that I had to have help doing *everything*. What a humbling experience to not have enough strength even to get out of bed without assistance.

I had a metal catch in my stomach with hinges (like you see on a mouse trap) holding together the metal and my stomach. That made it difficult even to turn over in bed without help, and sitting up was painfully uncomfortable without pillows supporting my back and arms.

For over a month I was bedridden, and during that time the volume of my voice dropped to barely above a whisper. With my voice almost on mute, with not enough stamina to pick up a piece of paper that fell to the floor, and with needing to wait for someone even to get me a glass of water, I struggled with my extreme limitations.

Christmas came just eight days after my second surgery. My sister Sarah, who at this time was one of the most sympathetic people in my life, had been concerned about what the holiday would bring for my husband and me. She knew family gatherings were very important to us and that earlier I'd planned to be with everyone in our extended family on Christmas Day. Sarah herself is always the life of the party when our families are together. My children always make sure she's invited when we have special celebration days, because she makes them laugh even while she's admonishing them to do right.

So on Christmas morning my sister called to wish us a Merry Christmas and to announce that she and her family were coming over to spend the day with us.

Now, I'm not usually abrupt; but as strongly as possible I said *no* to my sister. I said that if she wanted me to have a good Christmas, "then please do not come and don't allow your family to come. All I have strength enough to do is to lie in this bed and pray."

That shocked my sister and probably could have vexed her—like Reetie and Ruby vexed me. Thank goodness my sister knows how much I love her and knows I would never do anything deliberately to hurt her. She knew then just how sick I was.

After I told my sister to keep herself and her family away, my mind reflected on my two friends and their sicknesses. All those spoiled feelings I had for Reetie and Ruby became feelings of empathy and sympathy for what they had gone through. I finally understood that really sick people can't deal well with visitors. They're too sick and weak and uncomfortable to entertain or be entertained.

It was actually two months before I welcomed a few visitors. Even then they tired me out if they stayed more than an hour.

I later told Reetie that I finally got the point of her seclusion. Ruby, however, is with Jesus, so I couldn't tell her. (She might know anyway.)

Walk in Their Shoes

Yes, experience is an able teacher. And sometimes it seems to be the only way we're able to learn.

Many years ago, my husband and I were in dire financial straits. Earlier we'd made a lot of money as entrepreneurs in our separate businesses, but during an economic slowdown we encountered unforeseen events that upended both our situations. We lost almost everything we had.

At one point in those days I went to one of my best friends, who knew about our circumstances, and asked her to give me half of the six hundred dollars her company owed me so I could pay a bill. Her response was no. That stunned me, but I didn't fuss. I just left it alone.

Some years following, this friend experienced a similar financial dilemma as she struggled unsuccessfully to find a new job. After a lengthy spell of lacking money, she came to my home and told me this: "Thelma, when you asked me for half your fee and I refused you, I didn't understand. I assumed you were not doing all you could to get on your feet. Please forgive me for not understanding. You have to walk in other people's shoes before you can know what they're going through."

I know I've been characterized as "strange" because I can be happy in spite of life's circumstances.

She was discovering what I had discovered: Experience is an able teacher.

Get Out of Judgment Mode

The Lord tells us to judge not, or we will be judged. It's imperative that we get out of judgment mode—always sizing people up—and instead come to grips with the fact that people always have a reason for the way they act or react, a reason that makes sense to them.

More often than not, our judgment of others is incorrect. Just like my friend whose company owed me money, we assume we know what's going on with someone else. When will we ever learn?

I have been just as judgmental as the next person. There have been times when I met someone who wasn't bubbly and friendly, and I thought they were stuck-up. Later, when I got to know them better, I realized their personality was just quieter than mine. Not everybody's going to act like me!

I've also met people who were over-the-top friendly and talkative, and I assumed they were authentic and aboveboard—only to find out later they were a bit shady.

I wonder how many people have had misconceptions about me? I know I've been characterized as "strange" because I can be in my own world, trusting a living God, believing His every word, singing His praise every day, being happy in spite of life's circumstances—and not be disturbed in the least if nobody understands me.

It sure would save us a lot of unnecessary stress and bridge building if we would get beyond our narrow perspectives on the expressions, comments, circumstances, and behaviors of others, and instead get all the facts about people and their environment before we put them in our paper bags of judgment and fold them up in the crevices of our minds.

The Word of God tells us to judge *ourselves* (1 Corinthians 11:31, 2 Corinthians 13:5, Galatians 6:4). We must first see what's going on in our own lives and hearts, and surrender all that is not of God to Him, so we can have the privilege of His abundance.

But too often in self-judgment we pronounce the same wrong sentence on ourselves that we try to put on other people. Have you ever thought you were unworthy of something great? Have you ever been afraid of speaking up about what's right because you might get ostracized? Have you ever felt nobody wants to be in your presence because you're dull and have little to contribute? Have you ever condemned yourself for anything?

Perhaps we would benefit from the experience of looking closely at our own lives, personalities, dreams, goals, temperaments, and attitudes, while making this simple request of God: "Show me myself." And once He does, we must ask Him to teach us how to deal with ourselves. Or maybe a better request would be to ask the Holy Spirit to direct us to a Scripture that describes how to be delivered from our own negative self-judgments.

I firmly believe that when we take a long, hard, truthful look at ourselves, we won't be so quick to judge others. And when we walk in others' shoes we can see how that shoe fits and refrain from getting caught up in our faulty assumptions.

I Thought I Knew Him

We don't really have the right to make assumptions about others until we walk the same walk. After all, there really are so many things that we don't fully comprehend.

I really thought I knew Jesus. It was only while experiencing convulsions of pain in my body that I could even partially feel the pain and agony Jesus felt when He was crucified on that old rugged cross. Before experiencing my critical illness, I loved God, I adored Jesus, I relied on the confidence I have in the Holy Spirit—but I really did not *know* Him. Yes, I loved Him, worshiped Him, praised Him, enjoyed intimacy with Him, accepted His peace and salvation, talked with Him, prayed to Him, trusted Him, and (for the most part) obeyed Him. But I didn't know Him like I know Him now.

And still there's so much more to learn! There are a bazillion things I don't comprehend about Him, and He can never be totally figured out. But I can *kinda* relate to His pain. And my relating to Him has opened my eyes to His love for me and His redemptive power over me.

I understand now that these surgeries were light afflictions to help me walk a piece of the way home with Jesus. I wonder what else is in store for me to help me learn more about Him—to help me walk in His path. I don't know the answer to that, of course. But what I *do* know is this: God is not through with me yet!

Chapter 3

HE PREPARES, AND HE PROVIDES

Here's something else I have learned: that if we keep our minds and hearts open to the Spirit of God and allow Him to speak to us, *He will.* He does not allow anything to come upon us that we have not been forewarned about, though we may ignore the "feelings" or "urging" or "signs."

It's just as Jesus promised: "My sheep hear My voice" (John 10:27).

A Bathtime Blessing

David once spoke about being "undignified" in his praise to the Lord (2 Samuel 6:21–22). Sometimes I find myself being very undignified in my praise as well.

You see, I do a lot of my praising in the bathtub. It's just something about the softness of the bubbles and the aroma of the candles that puts me in the mood to praise God. I sing and pray and listen to Him speak to me in my spirit.

One early morning I was praying and singing in the tub while the Lord and I were having our time together, when Jesus presented Himself to me in my mind's eye. He began to communicate with me. I did not know at the time that He was giving me a preview of coming attractions in my life.

He stood slightly bent over, holding a palm branch in His right hand and two beautiful containers in His left hand. In my spirit I immediately knew that these containers held frankincense and myrrh.

He never said a word but simply stood there and motioned slightly as if to say, "Take these from Me."

I opened my mouth and responded audibly, with all confidence and determination, "Yes, Lord, give them to me. I'll take them." (You'd better be *ready* for whatever you tell Jesus you'll take.)

I did not realize what I was truly receiving. I did not know that the coming months would bring some of the rockiest days of testing in my life. They would test the persistence of my prayer life and my praise.

After this experience in the bathtub, I mentioned what I had seen to my daughter Vikki. She researched for me the meanings of the palm branch. It symbolizes a soul winner. She also discovered much about myrrh and frankincense. Myrrh has been used in the treatment of cancer and other diseases. Myrrh is more astringent, antiseptic, disinfectant, bitter, and tonic than frankincense. Frankincense has been used in the treatment of bronchial and respiratory ailments and is more anti-inflammatory, blood vitalizing, and mentally uplifting than myrrh.

What did all this mean to me? I wondered. (Please keep reading. You'll find out.)

God Was Doing Something

During this same timeframe, I happened to notice an office suite available next door to my daughter Lesa's beauty shop. Until that moment I had absolutely no intention of renting an office suite for my ministry.

I am the founder of the Daughters of Zion Leadership Mentoring Program, and ladies of all denominations, backgrounds, and ethnic groups have graduated from the nine-session program. For five years these ladies had been meeting mostly in my home. But now, when I saw that available space next to Lesa's beauty shop, the thought came alive in my mind of moving the ministry to this location.

A time was scheduled for me to look over the space. Before my husband met me and the landlord at the building,

I prayed, "Lord, if this is another crazy idea of mine, and You are not the author of this transaction, please let my husband say, 'We can't do this.' If this is Your prompting, let him say, 'Yes, we can do this.'"

For one year He was going to teach me to really pray—then release me to pray for kings and queens of the nations.

Well, my husband said yes. The landlady told us definitely that she had never rented a space less than three years, but she leased this one to me for only one year. We decided to lease the space for a year on faith, not really knowing whether it would perfectly fit our ministry's long-term requirements.

I needed furniture for this suite, and the landlady showed me all the furniture I would want. I agreed to purchase it for a very fair price. But soon afterward I was in a hotel room in another city, preparing to speak for a Women of Faith conference, when the Spirit of the Lord spoke to my mind and said, "Do not touch that furniture from a den of thieves. I will provide for you." Wow! In obedience to God, I canceled the agreement to purchase the furniture. But what was I to do next?

When I arrived back in Dallas, a face kept coming to my mind. It was the face of Minister Sandra McGriff, a lady who owns an elegant antique store. I paid her a visit, though I was sure I could not afford the luxury of this fabulous furniture and all the trimmings.

I told Sandra what I needed for our rented office and expressed my doubt that I could afford what she had for sale. She reminded me that anything is possible with God. The bottom line to this conversation is that she completely furnished my office for the same amount of money I would have paid for the den-of-thieves furniture.

As one of my friends would say, "Look at God!"

Once our new place was furnished, God told me what to name it: Daughters of Zion Leadership Mentoring Program National Headquarters and Prayer Center.

Shortly thereafter, I was driving on the Dallas North Toll Road one sunny morning, listening to one of my favorite gospel artists, and the Spirit of God overwhelmed me again. God told me in my mind that for one year He would teach me to *really pray*—and after that, He would release me to pray for kings and queens of the nations. Listen to that! One year! God had never been that specific with me. And isn't it interesting He told me to call the office a prayer center before telling me He would teach me to really pray?

It was not one of my crazy ideas to rent that office space, nor was it an accident that the landlady leased the space to us for a year. God was doing something! (Don't stop reading. It gets better!)

Never Give Up on God

I was extremely tired and struggled to make my last few speaking engagements of the year.

Meanwhile, the signs were evident—but I did not pay them any attention.

My body was talking loudly to me, but I was not listening. It told me I was very tired, but I kept pushing. My indigestion was an every-meal ordeal. My blood pressure frequently registered high. Obesity was a factor. And I had severe muscle spasms every day. But no, I convinced myself I was just fine. After all, I was doing God's work and God would take care of me. That's true; He did take care of me—until He said, "Enough! Wake up and get real; you're dying, girl. But good health is possible."

This time, God had to speak to me in a different tone of voice than when He spoke in my mind the other two times.

He finally got my attention through a biopsy. Things were serious enough to merit the kind of surgery that many women say is the best thing they've done in their lives. Surgery was set for early in December 2005, and I set apart the following six weeks for my recovery. I just knew that by the end of January I would be up and running, and able to keep a schedule that included teaching my course called Biblical Template for Counseling Hurting Women at Master's Divinity School and Graduate School in Orange Beach, Florida.

God had another plan! He showed me that I'm not running my life; He is. He is in control!

The surgery on December 8 went as planned, and I was home in three days. We thought all was well. But soon I began to cough severely and to experience significant pain. This pain progressed and I went to the doctor. Infection had set in. He sent me home with antibiotics, and we thought this would take care of the situation. But my pain had increased to almost unbearable intensity when my daughter Vikki noticed that my sutures had burst and my intestines were exposed.

The pain was so excruciating that in the ambulance on the way to the hospital I asked the paramedic to please not try to find my vein, because I could not stand any more pain. "Please," I cried, "no more pain, no more pain." Then I cried to Jesus, "O Lord, I can't stand it anymore!" At that very instant I fell asleep.

Let me stop right here and shout "Hallelujah!" God knows how much we can bear. Whether it's physical pain, emotional anguish, broken relationships, financial disaster, fresh grief, mental instability, church upheaval, or whatever your situation, never give up on God! He is always there when you need Him.

Not only did I sleep in the ambulance, but I slept through the surgery, and being in the critical intensive care unit, and being on life support…the entire event. I don't remember anything that happened, including my lungs collapsing—the reason for the life support. That's how good God is. He will cover your soul from tremendous agony, just like He will give you peace in the time of a storm.

All this was actually harder on my family, especially my husband of forty-four years, than it was on me. My children were troopers! They prayed and believed that I would be well. They remembered what God had promised me only a month earlier, when He said He was going to teach me how to really pray for one year. Their faith was so strong in the Lord, and they knew that because He had made this promise to me, He was not ready to take me to my heavenly home.

From the reports I later heard from friends in the waiting room, my children trusted in God and held their father together the entire time. And I was never afraid during either surgery. I had total peace. (Keep reading; I've learned a lot during this eventful journey.)

More Rough Stuff

One day during my recovery time in the hospital, I was given some kind of medicine that sent me on a hallucination trip that must be a sample of what the lake of fire and torment will be like after the Great White Throne judgment. (I'm just glad I have received Jesus and won't be there with the nonbelievers.) In my mind, this trip had me running away from pink bunny rabbits, pink cap pistols, and pink peanut patties. (Go on and laugh, it's okay.) I was trying to jump straight up from my bed to the ceiling in order to leap over these terrible objects that were trying to kill me. My husband later told me I was fighting for my life, trying to get out of the bed and saying, "I'm going to die here. Let me out of this bed!" Anyone who knows me realizes I must have been out of my mind. I would never act like that!

This experience taught me another lesson. I would never condone the committing of a crime, but now I can see how people who are on a trip like I experienced can commit heinous crimes and never realize it.

Not only did I go on that trip, I had respiratory problems and circulatory problems. They removed a malignant polyp, and I had to have a blood transfusion. Oh yes, it was rough!

But God had already shown me—on that morning in the bathtub when I accepted the gifts of the soul-winner's symbol (the palm branch) and the beautiful containers of frankincense and myrrh—that He had already given me the remedy for what I was going through.

Thank You, Jesus! You're the center of my joy!

(Don't stop reading; here come the miracles.)

The Lord Is My Provider

I don't have medical insurance. Perhaps you don't either. When you're self-employed, it's difficult to get good insurance that doesn't cost an arm and a leg. So rather than paying more than $700 a month just for me to be insured, my husband opted to save that money for a rainy day and not give it to the insurance company.

Just before my first surgery, when the hospital financial personnel asked me how I was going to pay for the charges, I said, "I don't have insurance, but I have the assurance that God will pay this bill."

Thank goodness we had saved the rainy-day money and were able to pay off the first hospital bill and each of the doctors.

Of course we did not anticipate the second surgery. But I continued to know and speak the fact that I had assurance from God, even if I did not have insurance.

After being home several days I received the hospital bill for the second surgery. When I looked at it I started to panic and get angry, but I remembered that *God is my Provider.* (I'll share with you lots more about that later in this book.)

I picked up the telephone and held the following conversation with the financial office.

"Hello, I'm Thelma Wells, and I'd like to talk to someone about my bill."

"Yes, my name is [whatever] and I'll be glad to help you."

"I just received my hospital bill, and I'm calling to tell you that I am not paying this bill."

"Excuse me?"

"I'm going to let you all refigure this bill, because you didn't send me the correct bill. Once I get the correct bill, I will be happy to pay you or set up payments with you. Would you please review it and send me a noninflated bill?"

"We'll see what we can do."

"Thank you and God bless!"

In a few days I got the corrected bill which was less than half of the first bill. Glory hallelujah! But I still didn't have the money.

I told Him I was depending on Him to pay this bill.

I held that bill up toward heaven and reminded God that before the foundation of the world He knew I was going to have two surgeries one week apart, and He knew what the bill was going to be. I boldly made my petition to Him and asked Him to pay the bill before the date that it would revert to the original amount. I told Him that I was depending on Him to pay this bill.

Praise always follows a request in my heart, so I just started singing and praising God for what He was about to do in my life.

Listen to this: The following Monday I received in the mail a retirement statement from an investment I had made years ago. I had not paid any attention to it for years. I would always give this kind of mail to my husband to handle, but this one I decided to open.

Lo and behold, the statement amount was almost exactly the amount I needed to pay the hospital in full. I started shouting and giving thanks to God. (Go ahead and shout with me!)

God is the God who keeps His promises. And His Word declares that He shall supply all we need according to His riches in glory from Christ Jesus (Philippians 4:19).

When I called the investment company to ask if I could cash in my retirement without penalty, they said I had absolutely no problem because I'm over the withdrawal age. After filling out the papers to get the check, we received the money in time to pay off the hospital before the interest started.

GLORY! God made it possible for me to pay the bill in full before the deadline. What a Savior You are, Jesus! God is a miracle worker!

Only a Light Affliction

All of God's miracles are mighty. But more than the messages from God and the miracles of God, what was really significant for me was the foremost lesson I learned from God about knowing Him.

I believe all Christians practice religion in one way or another, but my story has taken me far beyond religion to a relationship with Jesus that is more intimate than anything I have never known.

As I've said, I learned I did not really know God like I thought I did, though I've been a Christian for more than sixty years. I've taught Bible studies, Sunday school, and at Master's Divinity School and Graduate School. I speak for Women of Faith, the largest Christian women's conference in the world, and have experienced occasions where God moved in such marvelous ways. I loved God, trusted God, believed in God, was available to God, and had surrendered to God—but I really didn't *know* God before last December 8 like I *know* Him now, after weeks and months of life-threatening illness and prolonged recovery.

I know that the excruciating pain I experienced was so bad that I would not want my worst enemy to experience it. Honestly, I'd have to think long and hard before I would volunteer to take this pain for anyone else. It was just that bad. But compared to the pain, agony, and humiliation of my Lord, my own pain was only a light affliction.

When I think of the flogging He endured that stripped the skin off His back, the crown of thorns pressed upon His head, the nails driven into His hands and the spikes into His feet, and the soldiers spitting on Him and pulling His beard, making fun of Him and driving Him on as He carried the old rugged cross up the hill—I can't help but cry tears of thanksgiving for what He withstood for me. He was not guilty of any sin. He was the God-man. He did not deserve that at all. He willingly did it for one reason: LOVE. It makes me want to tremble, tremble, tremble. He did it all for me; He did it all for us. And I can't help but praise Him! *What a Savior You are, Jesus. I love You more now than ever before!*

My prayer is that you will never have to endure what I did. But seriously, I wouldn't take nothing for my journey now!

Oh, I want to learn more and more about You, Lord. I thank You for bringing me to a point of knowing for myself that I need to listen to You when You speak, because Your words are sure. I know without a doubt that You will not put any more upon us than we can stand, regardless of what it is.

You've proven again and again that You speak peace to our souls. Your promises are sure. You promised to rebuke the devourer if we tithe. If we give, You will give back to us good measure, pressed down, shaken together, and running over. No, You did not say *when* you would give back to us, but thank You for the savings account that You keep intact until the time is right.

O Lord, thank You for loving us so much that You gave Your life for us through humiliation and grief, cruelty and horror, bitterness and obscenities against You. Thank You for allowing me to taste just a tiny sip of the cup of pain You bore.

Now I am able to testify of Your fullness and goodness to us. I am able to write about You with more clarity than ever. I can now empathize more compassionately with the hurting people I serve.

Looking Back

I have learned that there is absolutely nothing that I can't trust Jesus with, including my health. I actually know what Proverbs 3:5–6 means when it says, "Trust in the LORD with all your heart, and lean not on your own understanding; in all your ways acknowledge Him, and He shall direct your paths." I realize that we can plan, but God has a better plan because "the LORD directs the steps of the godly" (Psalm 37:23, NLT).

Those "directed steps" truly can include good health. "Good health is possible," as the Lord assured me, and I should have gotten the picture before I nearly died. It's amazing how much abuse our bodies can take. Well, God made them, and He allows us to go and go until we reach a breaking point. Or at least that's what happened to me.

For sixty-four years I've been busy doing things that call for physical, mental, and spiritual exertion. When I was a "YP" (young person) my body could bounce back and heal itself in little or no time. As I got to be an "MP" (middle-aged person) I was too busy to notice that rest was really good for the body. Now that I'm an "OP" (older person), I finally get the picture.

Twenty-five years of traveling all over the world, including the last ten years traveling with the Women of Faith Conferences throughout the United States and Canada and visiting Third World countries without eating properly and resting enough caught up with me like a bombshell.

My health literally exploded in my hands, and the only logical place to go was to the hospital, then bed rest for months. Only the unction of God directed me to alternative medicine when my body was shutting down almost to death.

Thanks be to God, He directed me to Dr. Patricia Kirk of Houston, Texas. I was introduced to Dr. Kirk by way of my sister Sarah…who directed me to her sister-in-law, Linda…who told me about *her* sister-in-law—Dr. Kirk—who was an herbalist specializing in cancer. That was what I needed to hear. After getting permission to call Dr. Kirk, I contacted her at once.

I'll always remember our conversation over the telephone. As we talked about my medical problems, she asked pertinent questions to get a perspective about what was going on. Then she said, "I will work with you as long as you work with me and you do everything I tell you. If you don't do everything I tell you, I can't be responsible for what might happen. Do you hear me? I'll work with you—but you've got to work with me."

Her spirit and mine resonated, and I believed in my heart that Dr. Kirk was the physical answer that I needed to my health problems, though I knew God was the ultimate Healer. We started working together. In order to trace my progress, I kept a play-by-play calendar of the results of my visits and phone calls to the doctor, the herbs and dietary supplements I was taking, the amount of water I was drinking, the foods I ate, and the amount of rest I was getting.

I also followed her recommendation to call Dr. Michael Williams in Dallas. With the help of these two physicians, I'm healthier today than I've been in years.

Everybody's different. That means you cannot measure your health by mine, or your progress by my progress. You have to listen to your own body and love what your body tells you.

And I can assure you that if you get the right food supplements, drink a lot of water, get some needed rest, and laugh a lot—and if you pray the Word of God and praise and worship Him—you will get healthy.

CHAPTER 4

A PATH TO HUMILITY

I once read a book describing the journey of a man of God whom the Lord told to never lose his cloak of humility. In his journey, this man was challenged to go through twelve doors. He traveled through eleven of them with humility as his covering. But after he got through the twelfth door his comment was, "Look at what I've done!" This displeased God—and the man had to begin his journey all over again with door number one.

When I read that, I cried out to God and repented of any lack of humility I had. I asked God to take away everything that would cause me to be haughty and prideful, because having a consistently humble spirit had become a desire of my heart. I wanted the kind of humility that would take me to high places, to meet people in high places, and to work for Him in high places...but never, NEVER forgetting to cover myself with the cloak of humility.

Humility is so important because the Bible says, "Pride goes before destruction, and a haughty spirit before a fall" (Proverbs 16:18). I have to say that throughout my life I mostly never thought of myself as being prideful or haughty. To my knowledge, my friends did not think of me like that either. Many of them told me how humble I was to have accomplished so much without ever losing the common touch.

I've always wanted to be a personable person and enjoyed being warm, inviting, hospitable, delightful, and charming at the same time. (No brag, just fact.) Some of my travel companions tell me I'm *too* approachable, and that I never know when to stop grinning and talking with people who come up to me after my speaking engagements—even with those I meet in hotels, airports, stores, and various other places. I tell my travel companions that I'm just like that; I enjoy people and helping them any time I can. My goal is to travel globally teaching people how to fly like the bumblebee and defy the odds in their lives.

So at times I abruptly asked my travel companions to "shut up" (oops, a bad word) and leave me alone. I could never turn away from people who want to talk to me. I'm there to help!

PRETTY DARN CUTE

Now that I've had major health issues, my friends use that as a manipulation tool in their continuing efforts to protect me.

They say they're just trying to keep me alive and healthy. Okay, I'm starting to believe them. As they would tell you, I'm hardheaded. Is that considered prideful and haughty? I don't think so.

As all those health issues caught up with me, it was so difficult for me miss speaking at conferences, going to my book tables, and ministering to people, especially with the Women of Faith conferences. I wanted to be there. I wanted to be a part of the conference. I wanted to hear all the speakers. I wanted to go to the receptions. I wanted to be seen and to see other people.

Is *that* a haughty spirit? Is it pride? Goodness, I don't know. I never saw it that way. I viewed it as commitment to working for the kingdom...working on my assignment from God...doing God's work.

Whatever it was and is, for a year of my life I got a rude awakening. You see, I really had "prided" myself on never being seriously ill, never being in the hospital except to lose weight when I was nine years old. That's when I was so fat that I was put in a children's hospital to reduce me to my normal weight. It worked until I had my first child. Then, baby, something happened to my genes, and they extensively expanded to unhealthy proportions.

But I never really thought particularly that I might be overweight until I asked for a copy of my health records from my retiring internal medicine doctor, who had been seeing me for twenty years. When I read where he called me "morbidly obese," I wanted to hit him. After all, I looked in the mirror several times a day and had never seen what he was talking about. Maybe I was morbidly obese to him, but I was not morbidly obese to me.

After that, I would wonder occasionally if other people saw me like he diagnosed me—but this thought would quickly fade into the sunset. If my family thought I was morbidly obese, they never acted like it. In fact, I didn't notice anyone else acting like I was morbidly obese. So what did that doctor know? He was going by a chart, not by how I looked. In fact, I thought I looked good in my clothes and was pretty darn cute.

I thought I looked good in my clothes and was pretty darn cute.

Okay, is that haughty and prideful? If I was prideful a bit, my husband can be credited with helping me feel the way I did. He always told me I looked good to him. He also told me how smart I was and how he likes smart women. He always complemented me on what I did, how I did it, and how great I looked doing it. (Yeah, he's the man!)

My kids did the same thing. If I brought up my weight issue, they would say things like, "Mama, you look good, what are you complaining about?" You see, baby, sometimes I would not think as highly of myself as I should have, especially when I was exposed to skinny young thangs, and I was not feeling the best.

So, if I was prideful and haughty I didn't realize it, 'cause I got it straight from the mouths of the people I most loved and respected. They love me, too. (Do you think love is blind?)

Seeing Something Different

Then I got agonizingly sick, and agony has a way of humbling you—or at least humbling me! A year of illness and recovery will make you think again about being invincible—all that and a bag of chips, wonderful, and even cute. But it ain't cute being real sick.

I was stuck in the house for nearly five months. And in those months I looked in the mirror and saw a different person. I saw a person who had been humbled by the experience of other people having to do everything for me. *Everything* means EVERYTHING humanly possible that they could do, including bathe me. That's not cute!

And as I mentioned before, if I dropped a piece of paper on the floor, I had to wait until someone came into my room to ask them to pick it up. That ain't cute either! Thank goodness I could lift my hand and feed myself. That left a little dignity for me.

So if you hear anyone say they're glad to be sick, call the funny farm on them. They've become loony-toons and need mental attention. I'm not playing! I cannot imagine people enjoying being sick unless they are out of their minds.

No, I did not like being sick; I despised being afflicted for so long. My life changed from a happy, eventful, family-oriented, traveling, speaking, fraternizing existence to a sharp STOP EVERYTHING existence. My saving grace was the grace of God alone, expressed through so many people.

Nearing the seventh month of my affliction, my husband gave me another compliment: "You know, if you were not the woman of God you are, I don't believe you would have made it through this without being angry, bitter, and blaming God for all that's happened to you. You are a blessing to me—to watch you go through this more in love with God than before." Isn't he sweet?

I had thought about that myself. I had marveled at the miracles of God that showed up during this time of affliction. I learned so much about Him and me. He allowed me to walk just a *tiny* step in the kind of agony that Jesus must have known on the cross, and as a result I was given and blessed with so much.

Miracle After Miracle

Miracle after miracle was being displayed before my eyes. Let me explain what kind of miracle I'm talking about—not the sensational manifestation of a phenomenon or the unbelievable drama that is sometimes reported. No, just the lessons of truth that were revealed to me by God, lessons that I wouldn't have experienced unless I was down and could not get up. God knows what we need to elevate us to where He wants us to go. Prolonged sickness is indeed pure agony, but in the face of that agony He taught me real humility.

At present as I'm writing to you, seven months after my surgeries, I have not been released to drive a car more than five miles away from my house. Yes, I too asked why. My doctor's answer: "Mrs. Wells, I'll tell you when you can drive. Driving is very stressful, and we want you to avoid as much stress as possible until you completely heal."

And then, just as I thought I was healing completely, I discovered I'd developed severe arthritis and bone degeneration in my back. I had horrible pain again and got grounded like a disobedient child. This pain again put me in time-out from speaking and traveling. *Okay, Lord, enough is enough!*

Does that sound like humility to you? It was just a cry for complete healing! However, the miracles did not cease.

Even sitting here in this chair in arthritic pain, I've continued to enjoy the kind of fellowship with God that I began to experience in such a stronger way after my first hospital experience. I've found that He and I have such an interesting intimacy. I tell Him what I think and how I feel, and as a part of our covenant, I give back to Him His Word. He speaks to me in a still, small voice in my mind and heart, and He alerts me of impending situations.

I told you earlier how, prior to my afflictions, He showed me (in my mind) containers of frankincense and myrrh. After I found out their medicinal properties, I was amazed that in the beginning of time, God had perfected everything to heal and cure us. There's nothing new under the sun.

Well, as I sit here, I'm now the benefactor of the medical use of myrrh; I take it daily in capsule form, and also anoint myself daily with frankincense and myrrh oil. When I do, I seem to sleep more restfully at night than when I don't.

Another miracle is that I learned so much about empathy. In the past I've often said to someone, "Girl, I empathize with you on that." In reality, I did not have a clue about what Girl was going through. Now I understand so much better, because of all that *I* have gone through.

I especially have more empathy for people who are out of their minds, after my experience I told you about of that hallucination trip in the hospital (from too much pain medicine), when strange pink rabbits and peanut patties and cap pistols were chasing me and trying to kill me. Lord, have mercy! Evidently He did, because I did not hurt somebody while trying to jump straight up out of that bed and get above those murderers who were trying to kill me.

Today, as a result, I still do not condone any foul play, or the tragedies they cause, or any disobedience of the law, or any hurting of one's family or friends—but I *do* understand how those things can happen to those who are influenced by drugs. After all, I actually thought I was going to die, and I was only trying to protect myself. (So don't take anything that could alter your mind, without the supervision of a medical professional.)

God also performed a miracle in the ambulance when I was taken away for the second emergency within seven days of the first surgery that went bad. In that vehicle I cried out to God, "Lord, I can't take anymore!" God immediately put me to sleep without the aid of medicine because my veins were too weak to take a needle or anything else. As I told you, I slept through surgery, intensive care, life support, my lungs collapsing, and the entire ordeal until after I was transferred to a hospital room. God protected me from the mental anguish of this event. What a miracle!

Yes, you can slow down and smell the roses a lot better after you have known affliction. People who are around me say that it took this intervention from God to show me how to reduce my speed and relax. They consider it a miracle now to see me shut down from working as soon as I feel a bit tired, or when I'm not overly concerned about doing everything I thought was expected of me from my family, church, and community. They see how my house is no longer immaculate—just tidy—and that, to them, is also a miracle. They observe me not worrying about going places and doing things. They watch me watch what I eat and know that I am content on the food restrictions and dietary supplements I take daily. They notice how calm I am about things that used to be concerns for me, and they're amazed.

They're right. I see the miracle in what God's doing for my longevity on the earth. I've said through the years that I am going to live to be 120 years old and in good health. And such a miracle may be the truth, since I'm learning more and more how to take care of this temple of God, my body.

Stop Being Stupid

I believe the greatest miracle came when I was at my lowest ebb. I had cried and whined several days about not being any use to anyone anymore. I had cried because I could not attend my own Daughters of Zion Leadership Mentoring Program in February 2006 as I had intended. (This retreat is held the first weekend of February each year for those who are interested in going through the program, those who have completed the program, and people who only heard about the program by word-of-mouth or our marketing efforts.) Instead of being there, I was on time-out in the bed.

About 3 a.m. one night I got up and walked into my living room feeling almost defeated because I so badly wanted to be there with my Daughters of Zion. As I was crying, the still small voice of the Lord spoke to me again in my mind and heart, but He was not so nice. The first thing He said was, "*Stop being stupid!*"

What? I didn't even know God would talk to you in that tone of voice. Oh well, He's God and He knows what He's doing. He got my attention (consider that a miracle too).

This is the whole message He gave me: "Stop being stupid. Do you know who you are? You are My child. When I died for you on Calvary and rose on the third day, I got up with the keys to the kingdom in My hands. These keys are for you. You stand at an open door; all you need to do is to open that door and walk in."

I received that impartation. I understood what God was talking about. I knew He was telling me that my healing had *already* been completed when Jesus died and arose, having conquered death, hell, and the grave, as He promised in Scripture's prophecy:

> I will ransom them from the power of the grave;
> I will redeem them from death. O Death, I will

> be your plagues! O Grave, I will be your destruction! (Hosea 13:14)

I understand so much more fully now the meaning of this familiar description in Scripture of our suffering Savior:

> He is despised and rejected by men, a Man of sorrows and acquainted with grief. And we hid, as it were, our faces from Him; He was despised, and we did not esteem Him. Surely He has borne our griefs and carried our sorrows; yet we esteemed Him stricken, smitten by God, and afflicted. But He was wounded for our transgressions, He was bruised for our iniquities; the chastisement for our peace was upon Him, and by His stripes we are healed. (Isaiah 53:3–5)

These Scriptures (and more) saturated my mind and overflowed my soul. They gave me a new lease on life, a new anchor to hold on to. They renewed my strength and brought my attention to the wonderful privileges God had given me during this trying season of my life.

No, I could not go places, but I could look out of my windows and see the breeze blowing in the trees, the sun shining brightly from the sky, and the green grass; I could sense the silence of a quiet neighborhood and hear the birds singing in the trees. I could enjoy the sermons and songs on the television and radio that inspired and encouraged me and were so uplifting to my soul. I could appreciate all the people who were nursing and nurturing me, and I had a great appreciation for them and the time and energy they expended for me. I was better able to fathom the love-attention God gives all of us daily, whether we acknowledge Him or not.

Yes, my eyes were opened to the keys of healing I held in my hands, and I opened the door for God to move.

Chapter 5

LEARNING TO PRAY

ll my life, it seems, I've been asked to pray with and for people, and to teach them to pray. This has been a part of my calling.

Mandy: How Could God Allow This?

Mandy was sitting on the couch in my living room, sobbing and venting about her past life and her present dilemma. She said she was a Christian who reads her Bible, prays, and tries to treat everybody right, but life wasn't going in the direction she wanted it to. It never had.

Mandy was adopted as a child, and when her adoptive family finally had a natural child of their own, they decided they didn't want her anymore. She lived in foster homes and orphanages from the time she was a small girl until she became old enough to live on her own.

Actually she had done a good job of living on her own. She did well in school and educated herself with a college degree that landed her a position in a bank. Taking care of herself was one thing she could take pride in. She was careful to give God credit for helping her all along the way. Her problem was not that she did not believe in Jesus; rather, she wondered how God could allow her to go through all the tough things she had experienced in her short twenty-four years on this earth. She prayed, but she wondered if she was praying correctly and if God really answered every prayer. If He did, He sure was slow in answering hers.

Mandy's request to me was this: "Mama T, please teach me how to pray and get my prayers answered."

Bob: How Could God Be So Cruel?

Bob lost his mother a couple of months before his high school graduation. He had believed in God and begged God to keep his mother live so she could see him graduate. When she died, he could not believe God could be so cruel. What kind of God would take your mother before you graduated? Was it too much to ask that she live just a few more weeks? If God is good like people say, why did He take his mother?

Bob lived with a hatred of God that exhibited itself in his behavior while working at the many jobs he eventually lost, in his family relationships which became estranged for several years, in his disrespect for authority, and in his smoking, fighting, and totally rebelling against God and society. Bob was mad and confused.

In our conversation and my efforts to bring him back to the only person who could help him—Jesus—Bob resented my efforts and told me he didn't have a need to pray to someone who did not care about him. He refused to talk to someone who might not even exist. God had disappointed him once, and He would probably do so again.

"Mama T," he said, "I ain't gon spend my time talking to an unfair God. And anyway, I don't even know how to pray." He was asking me, in so many words, to teach him how.

Daisy: Wanting Integrity in Leadership

My friend Daisy had been a member of her church for a number of years and was an elder and officer when she discovered major discrepancies in the finances of the church. When she and others inquired about this to the pastor, they were accused of causing trouble in the congregation and harassing the pastor. There was no explanation given and no apology for the misuse.

Eventually the board discovered the manner in which the pastor had been misusing the funds. They approached the pastor and got nowhere with him. They took praying people with them, and still got nowhere. Finally they went to the church with the proof of his mismanagement. What the board received in return was to get put out of their church, stripped from their official licensing, and made the object of public ridicule.

Daisy called me, crying and upset. She told me she was so hurt and angry that she and the others who were ousted did not know how to pray for this pastor or that situation.

"Mama T," Daisy said, "help me do the right thing, and show me how to pray for this man. I need to be restored, because I feel like leaving the faith."

Bobby: Persecution in Prison

Bobby was in prison and having a rough time getting along with his counselor there. This was not a big penitentiary for hardened criminals; it was a facility for drug abusers that provided counseling and help in how to handle life's problems without using mind-altering substances.

But Bobby's counselor was not a God-fearing man, and he was quite the tyrant. Each time Bobby's parents would send their son something inspirational or spiritual to read, the counselor would get angry and put Bobby on restrictions. Being a man, Bobby would openly reject this outrageous conduct and end up in solitary confinement.

It was so hard for his family to believe that someone was so vicious as to punish Bobby for getting something that would help keep him comforted while away from home.

Bobby's mother was close to me, and she asked me to pray for Bobby and for the family. They were all distraught about this situation and knew it could get even worse for Bobby.

They asked me to pray that Bobby would speak the truth and that this situation would get better for him. They needed to know how to pray for their son.

A Self-Centered Couple

Donna and Donald were having marital problems even though they had been married for only a couple of years and had a lovely new baby. They were Christians and loved the Lord, but they could not get their lives on an even keel since their marriage.

As I began counseling them, I petitioned the Lord to find out what the problem was. Each time, the Lord would put in my spirit the word *self-centeredness*, but He would not let me speak that truth to Donna and Donald. This was a bit perplexing for me, because I wanted to cut right to the chase and tell them the problem.

For over two months I counseled them while listening to their sides of the story, speaking to them without taking sides, giving them Scripture to study together and to read separately, praying with them together and separately, praying for them privately, and offering them godly counsel.

Meanwhile they went up and down in their relationship. As soon as I thought we were making progress, one of them would get angry and lash out at the other. In spite of their effectual fervent prayers, they would be combative.

God still would not let me hit the issue head-on. That became even more frustrating for me. But I had to keep focus and keep praying for God's guidance and for Scriptures that applied to this circumstance.

From Tears to Trust

Yes, being called on to help others pray is a big part of my calling, and this has been shaped in my life from an early age.

When I was in kindergarten, my teacher, the late Mrs. Walker, would teach us that if we cried while we were praying God would know we were serious and would answer our prayers. I believed her, and I would cry every time I thought I wanted something. It was perplexing to not receive what I asked for all the time. So I cried harder the next time. It still did not always work as she said it would.

I cried harder the next time. It still did not always work.

I often wondered, "What's wrong with me? Does God really love me?" As I got older, the further teachings about prayer that I received in Sunday school saved the day for me.

I grew up in a praying house. We prayed about everything and always before we ate a meal. I was probably saying "Jesus wept" as my memory verse and prayer before I spoke the words "Mama" or "Daddy." Prayer was a staple. That's why it was so natural for my great-grandfather and me to play "Prayer Meeting," as I spoke about earlier.

When our circumstances were shaky, and money was funny, and the bills were due, I heard my great-grandmother begging God for our needs. And then I'd hear her singing songs: "Thank You, Lord," "His Eye Is on the Sparrow," "Sweet Hour of Prayer," "I Must Tell Jesus," and "Nearer My God to Thee," just to name a few.

I found out pretty early that crying was not assurance of an answer, but trusting in God's perfect will for my life was. I didn't know we were poor until I got grown. I always had the best clothes, shoes, and food, plus the best church, social, and cultural exposure of anybody in my neighborhood. Little did I know that my great-grandparents were asking God for provisions for me that we could not afford and did not have the resources for. But God is faithful, and He always delivers on His invitation to true abundance:

> Ho! Everyone who thirsts, come to the waters; and you who have no money, come, buy and eat. Yes, come, buy wine and milk without money and without price.... Listen carefully to Me, and eat what is good, and let your soul delight itself in abundance. (Isaiah 55:1–2)

My great-grandparents thirsted for that which was good for me and their family. They knew to go to the Water of Life and trust God, through the power of the Holy Spirit, for what they needed. They did not waste money on frivolous things but used their wages for things that were necessary for survival. They also knew that wine was good for the stomach and milk was good for the bones and that God was offering them the best that would help them live better. They listened to God, and their souls delighted in abundance.

In answer to my great-grandparents' prayers, people would give them opportunities for me to be a better person. Mr. Sanders paid for my summer camp every year. Mrs. Jackson and Mrs. Less kept me in the best clothes and shoes. My Aunt Allene and Uncle Jim exposed me to the best restaurants that black people were accepted in. My church had trips all over Texas and other states, and we enjoyed outings where we fellowshipped with other congregations.

My grandfather, Daddy Lawrence, took me to movies and plays and the symphony. We would go to art museums and aquariums. None of this was paid for by my great-grandmother. She thirsted, asked, sought God, and knocked at the door, and God answered her prayers. She was actually praying God's will because He wants us to have the best and be exposed to the best of His creation.

I learned a lot of prayer lessons from the angels who raised me. Even when I got ready to go to college and realized they could not afford to send me, I saw my granny petition God, and He answered her prayer through Mrs. Less, the lady she worked for. Because of Granny's thirst for the abundance of God in life, I was able to get a bachelor of science degree in education from the University of North Texas. Her faith in God's promises inspired me to always trust in the Lord and not try to figure everything out, because He would direct me in the right path if I would only allow Him to.

Sharing with God

You may be asking, "How can I pray when I'm not even sure I know what prayer really is?"

Someone has called prayer "the heart's sincere desire—unspoken or expressed."

Prayer is communicating with God, sharing with God your dreams and desires, listening to God for answers to your prayers, calling on God when you are in distress, and thanking God for His goodness to you.

Prayer is opening up and expressing to God exactly what you feel about a situation—even if it means yelling at God—as you try to understand your heartaches and disappointments.

It's so much easier talking to God than talking to a person. A person like me might take your sentence and try to tell you what you're trying to say. If someone is having a hard time saying something, I'm tempted to take his or her sentence and run with it. But God will never do that!

A person may misinterpret what you're saying to them; God never misinterprets. In fact, He already knows what you need before you ask. Therefore, you're safe talking to God about *anything.* He will hear and answer your prayers. And God's answers are always for our good!

Helping Others Through Scripture and Prayer

If you are looking for some Scriptures to pray over your circumstances, let me share with you what I shared with those people I mentioned at the beginning of this chapter.

Mandy

With Mandy—the young woman who was weeping on the couch in my living room—I shared Psalm 27:10: "Though my father and mother forsake me, the LORD will receive me" (NIV). I had to pray with her to help her understand that though her parents and others had forsaken her, God never did. In fact, He is the one who encouraged her heart to complete her education. The Holy Spirit living within her had kept her from going crazy.

As we prayed, I asked her to picture Father God in her mind and to ask Him to speak to her spirit and tell her what He wanted her to know. After some time of consecrated prayer, I saw a smile of relief on her face. She was then willing to tell me what she had heard in her mind from God. She said He told her everything was going to be all right and that He loved her. I knew it had to be God, because God will always speak His Word. You can check it out in the Scriptures.

Bob

Bob, the young man who had lost his mother before his high school graduation, was a more difficult nut to crack. His hatred of God convinced me that he had never accepted Christ as his personal Savior. After asking him if he believed in Jesus, he admitted that he thought He was a good person, that's all. So we were at square one. After a lengthy discussion about who Jesus is and how He came to save all people from their sin and how Jesus wanted to come and live in his heart and help him deal with the pain, I finally read to him John 3:16. He prayed with me to receive Jesus and admitted he still did not know how to pray.

I responded, "Do you know how to talk?"

A little shocked at my response, he answered, "Sure!"

"Well," I said, "if you can talk you can pray. Just open your mouth and tell God whatever you need to tell Him, or ask Him whatever you need to ask Him."

I explained that praying is talking to God and listening to Him with your mind for an answer. We then practiced just talking to God the same way Bob talked to me. It would take some practice for him to learn how to listen with his mind for God's directions, but this would come.

To date, Bob is growing in the knowledge of God by praying, occasionally reading the Bible, and watching God work in his life.

Daisy

Daisy was distraught about the situation with her pastor and church. I called her attention to Acts 8. The deacon Stephen had just been stoned to death (as recorded in Acts 7), and this had precipitated a great persecution against the believers, so that they were scattered far and wide. Saul (who later became the apostle Paul) was at this time trying to destroy the church, and seemed to be doing a good job of it. But even with all these terrible happenings as the background, the evangelist Philip carried on preaching and doing what God called him to do.

I suggested to Daisy that she keep on working for the kingdom in spite of persecution. I prayed for God to renew her mind and perfect her for the task God has given her, so she can win souls through personal service for the kingdom.

When I talked to her recently, she had found a new church home where she is serving the Lord with freedom under a powerful new pastor and a loving congregation.

Bobby

Bobby is the young man in prison. His case had to have some serious Scripture praying to resolve it.

A friend of mine told me to read 2 Chronicles 20 and 21, and wherever Jehoshaphat's name appeared in those chapters, we replaced it with Bobby's name. We read that after "Bobby" prayed, he began to sing praise to God. Praise changed the atmosphere and confused the enemy; the enemies killed off themselves, and "Bobby" was saved.

After five days of reciting these Scripture as prayer, the atmosphere in the prison changed. The enemy who was causing Bobby to be punished for trusting in the name of the Lord was removed, and the entire scheme for Bobby's downfall was overturned.

Donna and Donald

Donna and Donald had breached their marriage contract by not being truthful to each other. Because they were believers and had a working knowledge of how prayer works, I had them study marriage Scriptures and also, wherever it was appropriate, to put their names in the context of the passage. I told them to pray those words for their deliverance.

I had them study Isaiah 58 and apply the proper fast and prayer time so the breach in their relationship could be repaired. Even though they were reluctant to fast and pray as the Scriptures said, they said they would try it.

After a series of meetings, prayers, submission to each other, and fasting, they have begun a new and improved life of harmony and trust.

Prayer Is the Key

Prayer is the key to the kingdom and faith unlocks the door.

If you fall on your knees...He'll give your heart ease. He's always near, and He'll hear if you pray.

(If you want to learn more about prayer, I encourage you to turn to Special Section 2: "Secrets of Prayer," in the back of this book.)

Do You See the Everyday Miracles?

Perhaps you need to start with square one in your own life. Perhaps there really are everyday miracles going on in your life, but you simply are not aware of them as such. God wants to show you these things. He wants to talk to you in His still small voice and teach you something.

It's not hard to hear from God in this way when you have a relationship with Him. I'm not talking about religion or meditation or seeking your higher power; I am talking about a deep-down, sure-enough acceptance of Jesus as your personal Savior and making Him the Lord of your life.

He wants to talk to you in His still small voice and teach you something.

I'm talking about a free gift that is given to you just as you are. You may have lived a life of crime, drugs, and abuse, or done other horrible things; but God sees you as His creation needing to find your way to Him. And He has provided everything you need to find it!

You know, it was by God's grace that I was able to visit Ghana, West Africa, and one day while I was there, I was asked to go to the fetish priest. A fetish priest is one who sacrifices to animals, thinking that the spirits of animals have a power to create hexes and mysticism.

As I stood there and looked at that fetish priest, I thought about the Lord's power and how He had shed His blood on Calvary for that priest and for all of us.

I looked beside this fetish priest at the bones lying there from the carcasses of animals, and I said to the priest something like this:

"You know, you can have peace today. In fact, you never have to burn another animal in sacrifice, or shed any blood. Because the blood that was shed for you on Calvary was already spent to beg your pardon."

I said to him, "When the thorns were pressed onto Jesus' head, the blood that dripped from those thorns was dripped *for you.* When the nails were driven into His hands, the blood that flowed from His hands flowed *for you.* When the spikes were driven into His feet, the blood flowing from those feet was shed *for you.*

"No longer do you have to sacrifice to idols. Because indeed that blood bought you with a price on Calvary's tree. And you can have the blest assurance that He shed His blood *for you,* that He died *for you,* rose *for you* on the third day to bring *you* back into His eternal kingdom for which you were created."

What a blessed assurance to know that when we are in Jesus, we can walk through the valley of the shadow of death and fear no evil.

Maybe you've heard these words before: "For God so loved the world that He gave His only begotten Son, that whoever believes in Him should not perish but have everlasting life" (John 3:16). The blood of Jesus proves that Jesus loves *you,* and there's nothing you can do to deny or diminish that. He wants to give you not only eternal life with Him when you die, but also a richer, cleaner, more hopeful and powerful life right here on this earth. Did you know that Jesus said He came to give you life "more abundantly"? (John 10:10).

It's so simple to receive and enjoy these things. If you don't personally know God as your Creator, and Jesus as your Savior, and the Holy Spirit as your Guide—then this is a great time to ask Jesus into your heart to become Lord of your life.

You can pray this prayer to the Lord right now, wherever you are:

"Lord Jesus, I don't understand how You can do this, but I believe You can save me from my sins. I believe that God raised You from the dead and that You, Jesus, are alive in the world today. I'm asking You to come into my heart and become my Lord and Savior, and speak to me like You spoke to Thelma. I know that You are God, and I want to be Your child. I want to turn my life over to you. I want to be able to fully depend on You to help me in my time of need and to rejoice with me when I'm happy. I want the Holy Spirit to live inside me, helping me with all my issues. Thank You God for receiving me and accepting me into Your kingdom. Amen."

If you sincerely pray this prayer, then your wandering days are over. Jesus has come into your life, according to the promise in Romans 10:9 which says, "If you confess with your mouth the Lord Jesus and believe in your heart that God has raised Him from the dead, you will be saved."

It means you now have all the rights and privileges of all God's children, and the promise of life eternal.

PART II

...BECAUSE I KNOW THE I AM

Chapter 6

THE GREAT I AM

God said to Moses, "I AM WHO I AM";
and He said, "Thus you shall say to the sons of Israel,
'I AM has sent me to you.'"

Exodus 3:14, NASB

In a black church, a worship service has lots of emotion and expression. Some people call it noise; we call it "rejoicing in the Lord." The preacher says something that's right-on, and everybody shouts "Amen!" The choir sings a moving selection, and the whole audience will either sing along, or shout aloud, or cry, or stomp their feet, or clap their hands.

Such a stream of outbursts is expected by almost everybody who attends; it's surprising and startling only to those who've never experienced it.

But I remember one particular Sunday—I was eighteen at the time—when the current of expression was stilled.

There was a hush in our church sanctuary. Nobody was talking, singing, or demonstrating. It was like a trance had come over the people.

A Flow of Life

Before us, an artist was using fluorescent crayons to skillfully draw the crucifixion of Christ on a white canvas set upon an easel.

As the artist drove the nails through the hands of Jesus with his crayon, I was watching as real blood (so it seemed to me at the time) dropped from the Savior's hands. It was for me a vision of life—life flowing out of the hands of a Man who had never done anything wrong.

For me, the scene so captured the majesty of God and the willingness of His Son to become a scapegoat for me that I found myself standing up in the sanctuary (I was the only one standing) and shouting with a loud voice, "Yes, Yes, *Yes!*"

My "Yes" was in answer to the voice of God whispering in my ear something sweet and peaceful. I couldn't understand what He was saying; I knew only that this was the holiest experience I could ever remember having. I knew I was standing on holy ground.

I had never before studied about the Great I AM; I couldn't say that God had ever told me, as He told Moses, to take off my shoes because I stood on holy ground; but I knew I was in the presence of the Most High God.

Anyone in that kind of experience—in *His* presence—will recognize in their soul that He is the self-existent One in a way that no one or nothing else in all this world can ever be.

As I watched the artist closely, I continued shouting and crying and giving God all praise—"Yes God! Yes, God! *Yes, God!*" My shouts actually alarmed the church, and people later told me I kept going for quite a while. But I don't remember the length of time; I just know that in those moments I was in the presence of the Great I AM.

Who Is I AM?

I'm totally fascinated by the story of the eighty-year-old Moses as he came upon a burning bush while watching his father-in-law's sheep on a remote mountainside in the wilderness. It's as unforgettable for me as it was for Moses.

Imagine how you would have responded if, in the middle of the summer, you walked up to a bush that was burning but not burning *up*—flaming without charring or disintegrating—just burning! And only *one* bush! As orange and blue flames leaped up out of this green shrubbery without igniting anything around it, it must have been a stunning, overwhelming sight.

If you saw that, would you question whether you were losing your mind? Whether the heat might have gone to your head and cooked your brain? Humanly, I think so. But this was an ethereal experience for Moses, and I believe he sensed he was in the presence of a mighty being even before God spoke up and told him to take off his shoes.

I try to imagine being a bee in the breeze listening to their conversation:

> The angel of the LORD appeared to him in a blazing fire from the midst of a bush; and he looked, and behold, the bush was burning with fire, yet the bush was not consumed.
>
> So Moses said, "I must turn aside now and see this marvelous sight, why the bush is not burned up."
>
> When the LORD saw that he turned aside to look, God called to him from the midst of the bush and said, "Moses, Moses!" And he said, "Here I am."
>
> Then He said, "Do not come near here; remove your sandals from your feet, for the place on which you are standing is holy ground."
>
> He said also, "I am the God of your father, the God of Abraham, the God of Isaac, and the

God of Jacob." Then Moses hid his face, for he was afraid to look at God.

The LORD said, "I have surely seen the affliction of My people who are in Egypt, and have given heed to their cry because of their taskmasters, for I am aware of their sufferings.

"So I have come down to deliver them from the power of the Egyptians, and to bring them up from that land to a good and spacious land, to a land flowing with milk and honey, to the place of the Canaanite and the Hittite and the Amorite and the Perizzite and the Hivite and the Jebusite.

"Now, behold, the cry of the sons of Israel has come to Me; furthermore, I have seen the oppression with which the Egyptians are oppressing them.

"Therefore, come now, and I will send you to Pharaoh, so that you may bring My people, the sons of Israel, out of Egypt."

But Moses said to God, "Who am I, that I should go to Pharaoh, and that I should bring the sons of Israel out of Egypt?"

And He said, "Certainly I will be with you, and this shall be the sign to you that it is I who have sent you: when you have brought the people out of Egypt, you shall worship God at this mountain."

Then Moses said to God, "Behold, I am going to the sons of Israel, and I will say to them, 'The God of your fathers has sent me to you.' Now they may say to me, 'What is His name?' What shall I say to them?"

God said to Moses, "I AM WHO I AM"; and He said, "Thus you shall say to the sons of Israel, 'I AM has sent me to you.'"

God, furthermore, said to Moses, "Thus you shall say to the sons of Israel, 'The LORD, the God of your fathers, the God of Abraham, the God of Isaac, and the God of Jacob, has sent me to you.' This is My name forever, and this is My memorial-name to all generations." (Exodus 3:2–15, NASB)

Just Like God, and Just Like Us

Did you hear God? He told Moses, "This is My name forever!" God selected Moses—an Israelite adoptee to the queen of Egypt, a runaway murderer from the land of Egypt, a lowly shepherd who married a pagan black girl—to announce to the world that His name is *not* God (that's

His position); rather, His *name* is *I AM.*

And the I AM was taking Moses back to Egypt—back to where his family roots were and where his upbringing began—to lead God's people out of slavery.

Ain't that just like the God of the universe! To take such an unlikely human being and place him in a position of authority and leadership over hundreds of thousands of people, entrusting him to lead them out of anarchy and slavery.

Ain't that just like the God of the universe! To place such an unlikely human being in a position of leadership.

Of course, Moses tried to weasel out of this calling (as we read in Exodus 4) by telling God he had a speech impediment. God already knew that, of course; after all, He *made* Moses. So in reply, God described the plan He'd already worked out: Moses' brother, Aaron, could speak for him. Moses lost that argument before he even started it.

In the way Moses first responded to God's call, he was just like the average one of us. God tells us intimate and strange things to do and say. Then we try to make excuses for not obeying what He asked. God knows what we're trying to do, and sometimes He lets us think we're getting away with it. But there's always a reckoning day. In other words, you can run from God, but you can't hide. He will find you, and you will either get on up and go to your Egypt, like Moses did, or you will reject God and face the consequences. It's really that simple.

Smack-Dab in the Presence

I can remember a particularly memorable occasion when I clearly sensed I was in the presence of God as He communicated a vast and strange calling. A few years ago, Dr. Myles Munroe was ministering in Dallas, my home city. I went to the service and sat on the first row, in the end seat, on the left of the sanctuary.

As Dr. Munroe was preaching and ministering to the people, suddenly he looked over at me and called me out of my seat. He was speaking a prophetic word to me about how God was going to use me more in my latter days than in my prime, and how a worldwide ministry was going to thrive under the direction of the Holy Spirit.

Still turned toward me, Dr. Munroe raised his hands. Although he was standing about twenty-five feet away from me, I went out like a light—I kid you not.

I don't remember anything else that happened that evening, until after the service had been over for a while and someone was helping me off the floor. But I *can* tell you that while on I was on that floor, I was in the presence of the Great I AM. It was not a burning bush I saw, but I saw and heard Jesus.

He was speaking to me and assuring me that I was on a mission for Him, and that He would protect me by giving His angels charge over me to keep me in all my ways. The I AM told me (and when I speak of "I AM," Jesus is always included—you'll see why at the back of this book in Special Section 1: "Christ the I AM")—that He was my sustainer, my comforter, my healer, my stronghold, my helper, my controller, my protector, my joy, my everything—and that when I keep my trust in Him, I can do all things He has assigned me to do.

I fully experienced the realization that I was in the presence of I AM. The Almighty God spoke to me in my spirit and gave me the kind of courage I could not have received from anybody else.

I AM, as Moses learned, is God's name, and it means "the self-existent God." There's nothing in front of I AM and there'll be nothing left behind I AM. He is the Alpha and the Omega, the First and the Last, and no human being can ever work in the way He works.

That's why there are no words to fully explain how it feels to be smack-dab in the presence of the Lord. And it is why no one can define to the fullest what "the I AM" means. This book cannot begin to cover the immeasurable vastness of His name.

It's all ultimately unexplainable. But I do stand on the promises of God, whose name is *I AM,* and I declare to you that *I CAN…BECAUSE I KNOW THE I AM!*

Your Journal

Start a written record of what you're learning these days about the I AM. And begin by writing down your answer to this question: How can your own life change as you learn more about the I AM, and that He is always with you?

CHAPTER 7

I AM IS YOUR HEALER

For I am the LORD who heals you.

EXODUS 15:26

The majority of e-mails I get are requesting prayer for people who are sick—many of them critically. I've never seen the likes of so many people with what can be called fatal diseases. (Even apart from those diseases that are on the rise, we have enough pollution in the air and contaminants in our food to have already killed us all—were it not for the great immune system God gave us. I'm so glad we don't have to depend totally on medicine, potions, doctors, and hospitals to feel safe and act responsibly in the midst of all this.)

When I receive e-mails, letters, or phone calls from those who are ill, or when I speak with them face-to-face, I offer them Scriptures about healing, with my written comments.

(You can see these Scriptures and comments in Special Section 2 in the back of this book; you'll discover that God's Word has much to say about this.) My list of these is long, because the Lord has been teaching me to search His Word, to pray the Scriptures over every situation, and to watch Him keep His Word. I have experienced many situations where I needed to know this.

NOT NOW!

Several years ago I received a phone call from my sweet, soft-spoken doctor. She had read my mammogram results and wanted me to come into her office right away so she could talk to me.

My reply was, "No, baby, not now!"

She was insistent. But I was determined, and I continued to reply, "No, baby. I'll call you when I'm ready to come in."

Now don't think I was being rebellious or frightened. Not one bit. I needed to consult the Doctor who has never lost a patient and who has never given the wrong diagnosis—the Doctor of the Universe: Father God, and Dr. Jesus.

I asked God to direct me in what I should do about this lump in my breast. I wanted to do the perfect will of God in this situation. If He had prompted me to go to the doctor immediately, I would have gone. If I had sensed the peace of mind that surgery was necessary, I would have had the surgery. But I wanted to be certain I was doing what He wanted me to do.

It's amazing how God speaks. After praying for direction for a couple of weeks and not getting any leads from the Holy Spirit, I spoke at a ladies' tea in Dallas. There were several interesting speakers there, one of whom told about her lifelong journey with health problems and how she was healed from cancer and multiple sclerosis by following a natural health plan. I was moved—not by what she said, but by what she did: When she finished speaking, she stepped off the stage and made her way directly to me. She gave me her business card and said, "Miss, you need to call me because you need me." Well, that was a startling surprise!

I was laughing; I told her she was wasting my time and hers, because prayer changes things.

Curious about what she had to say, I called her early the following Monday and made an appointment to see her that day. When we were together, she explained more about her illnesses and healing, then suggested that I needed to do some similar things to what she had done.

Mind you, this woman did not know me, and I did not know her. I never told her about my brief conversation with my doctor regarding the mammogram. I simply listened to what she said—and started that very day on a regimen of cleansing, herbs, vitamins, and a change of diet. (Yes, I had to start eating healthy. Shucks!)

I did all of that, but the main ingredient in my approach was prayer and praise. I prayed that God would heal me. I reminded Him that He had assigned me a lot of work to do, and I could not do it as efficiently ill as I could in good health.

I'm so radical that I laid my hands on the area where the lump was and anointed myself with oil in the name of Jesus. I just followed the directions in our Guide Book (the Bible):

> Is anyone among you sick? Let him call for the elders of the church, and let them pray over him, anointing him with oil in the name of the Lord. And the prayer of faith will save the sick, and the Lord will raise him up. And if he has committed sins, he will be forgiven. (James 5:14–15)

There was only one thing in these instructions that I didn't do. I did not call for the elders of the church. I felt like the Great I AM was enough for me to call on.

Once I had followed these instructions in James, I turned to the Psalms:

> I will praise You with my whole heart; before the gods I will sing praises to You. I will worship toward Your holy temple, and praise Your name for Your lovingkindness and Your truth; for You have magnified Your word above all Your name. In the day when I cried out, You answered me, and made me bold with strength in my soul. (Psalm 138:1–3)

I've learned from experience that when you match prayer with praise, you receive power. I had the power to follow the dictates of God because it had to be Him who directed that lady to give me her card, which brought me to her, so she could teach me how to be healthy.

Now the real test would be when I called my doctor, and she told me to get checked again.

Within the next three weeks, I decided to call this doctor and return to her office for her consultation. This time, she told me to go back to the breast clinic for another mammogram.

I went in for the mammogram, and my technician was familiar with my case. After the test, she had me wait in the sitting area for the results.

When she returned, she asked me to take yet another mammogram, because the first one evidently did not take. I agreed.

After this additional test, she came back into the room and told me that I needed to take a sonogram, and explained the procedure and assured me of the doctor's pleasant bedside manner. I agreed.

However, the sonogram was not detecting that anything was wrong with me, and this was irritating the doctor. (So much for the pleasant bedside manner.) She blamed her lack of results on faulty machinery and ordered another sonogram machine. I just laid there smiling and singing.

The test with the new machine gave her the same results. By this time, the doctor was *really* irritated. She spoke harshly as she brought out the X-ray film that was taken weeks ago and told me to look at. I did. She asked me if I saw that spot. I did. She said to me, "I can't find it...and why are you laughing?"

I told her I was laughing because the lump was gone; she was wasting my time and hers, because prayer changes things.

She responded (with unpleasant bedside manner), "Get up and get your clothes on and get out of here."

I laughed again and got out of there. The I AM—the Healer—had taken my sickness away. Hallelujah!

Every year I get a checkup, because we cannot take anything for granted. But I know God is able to do much more than we can in all of our situations. I am cancer free at present, and many others can testify of being free from whatever has ailed them.

Now listen, I understand that other people's experience with cancer or other diseases or injuries will *not* necessarily have the same results mine did. My healing was not because I have some monopoly on good health; God doesn't love me any more than He loves everyone else. It was just not the perfect will of God in that time that I have cancer and be sick. But sometimes, in His perfect, loving will, He most certainly allows sickness to touch us.

One of the most wonderful men in my life, my father-in-law, was critically ill. We fasted, prayed, praised, and sought prayer from many people asking God to heal him of his ailments. Almost my entire family believed that God would raise him up and allow him more time on this earth. But the day he was released from the hospital was the day he died.

It was hard for one of my children to receive the news of this death because we all believed that if you prayed, God would give you exactly what you prayed for. So this was a rude awakening for some of the family. It took them a long time to reconcile with God's decision because they thought God had let them down by not keeping His Word as the Healer.

As time passed by and the words of God became clearer and clearer to them, they finally realized that even death is a part of God's healing process and the ultimate healing. For a Christian, it is the best healing ever, because afterward they will never again have to taste pain, sorrow, hurt, and discouragement. As my friend Kathy Tricolli says, "They pass from life to life."

Once we realized that God was at work healing all His children, we resigned ourselves to His perfect will. When a loved one dies in the Lord, the hardest part is that others must stay behind on earth without that person. We grieve for *us* and not for the one who has gone. (I feel sure that my father-in-law would be quite upset if he found himself back on this earth as it now is.)

God's Still, Small Voice

In mid-2005, only twenty-three days apart, both of my daughters had little girl babies. Lesa experienced no problems in her delivery, even though her baby was three weeks early. Vikki, on the other hand, experienced severe health problems.

When Vikki was admitted to the hospital, I received the news by telephone while I was driving home to Dallas. I had gone the previous day to Bluff Dale, Texas, where I was scheduled to teach a Bible study, but I found out after I got there that it needed to be postponed until the next month. I thank God that when I learned about Vikki, I was already on my way back and could get to the hospital within the next couple of hours.

When I arrived at the hospital, I discovered that my daughter was gravely ill with a variety of complications, including kidney failure. This was serious! I knew I would need to settle in and stay at the hospital with her through this ordeal. Her husband was there, but there's nothing like Mom being with you when you're sick.

My next couple of days (long ones!) were spent changing medicine containers that ran needles through tubes into my daughter's arms and hands, holding oxygen masks over her face, watching monitors mount up and down the scale on the machines, and watching the baby's heartbeat vary from normal to abnormal, dipping up and down toward the thick, red lifeline scale. Vikki's kidneys were not draining, and when I watched the distressed brow lines on the faces of nurses who came to check her catheter bag, I realized things were touch and go. My daughter's body was shutting down.

The prayer warrior in me was tearing down the walls of death as I sent word to hundreds of others to join me in prayer. The fight got so bad that in one of Vikki's awake moments, she started praying and pleading with God, "Oh, God, not now. Not now! Please let me stay and raise my baby!" She asked me to sing "Great Is Thy Faithfulness" and every other hymn or praise song I could think of. She began to recite Scripture; for hours she recited every verse in the Bible she could think of. We had our own little worship and praise period in that room.

Her poor husband did not realize how sick she was until later, because I would send him on errands for food and other things to keep him occupied. Much of Vikki's time awake was spent with just the two of us standing in the gap and depending on God for a change.

Several hours into this continuum, Vikki's doctor came in and told her she would have to deliver the baby at once because that was the only way Vikki would get well. The doctor explained the timeframe and process for the C-section, but Vikki would not hear of it. She had decided she was going to carry her baby full-term, and she was going to have it without surgery. After much discussion, the doctor suggested that Vikki get a second opinion, and Vikki agreed.

Another physician, a wonderful doctor who was the head of obstetrics, came to examine Vikki. As he was thumped on the wooden table next to her bed, he said, "Vikki, do you hear this?'

"Yes."

"Vikki, listen! This is the still, small voice of God telling you it's time for you to have this baby. If you wait until tomorrow or another day or so, you will have a stillborn baby. Listen to the voice of God, and not the voice of the enemy."

I knew this doctor was a Christian, and I knew he was right. So did Vikki. She said, "All right. I feel much better now. You said the right thing."

Twelve hours later, a healthy little girl was born and the mother and baby did well.

God Completes What He Begins

Did God heal Vikki just because people prayed?

I can't accurately answer that, because we cannot second-guess the actions of God. I do know that along with other people's prayers, Vikki herself was praying and asking for more time. I know that praise-singing was being lifted up in that room. And I know that God answers our prayers and rejoices over our praise.

The most fascinating aspect of this entire ordeal is that I got frightened only one time, for about five seconds. And then I returned my thoughts to Psalm 138, and I remembered further down the page where we read these words: 'The Lord will perfect that which concerns me" (Psalm 138:8). And I thought, *The Lord will perfect that which concerns Vikki.* I kept repeating this to myself and to Vikki as a confirmation of what God was doing in that place.

Sure enough, God moved on Vikki's body. Her kidneys began to function again just before they rolled her into surgery, where her healthy baby was born.

God walked with us through those several days and gave us peace, even when, physically, things were in turmoil. About two weeks later Vikki asked me how I managed to remain so calm when my daughter seemed to be dying. I told her that the Word of God kept echoing through my mind: "He will perfect what He started in Vikki." I knew that God was with us through the valley of the shadow of death. He had given me the strength I needed to stand firm on the foundation that God was in control and would do what was best for both Vikki and the baby. He gave me the calm assurance that we were not walking through this alone, for the Great I AM was cradling Vikki in His loving arms, while guarding my own mother's heart and also protecting the spirit of Vikki's husband, until this trial ended, one way or the other.

My family fully realizes that this event could have gone the other way. She *could* have died—because God does not heal everyone the way we want Him to. There may be some who would have us believe that every prayer for healing is answered with the sick person rising up and walking. No! We know that is not true. But for those of us whose hope is in the Lord, we know it *is* true that God will give us the strength, stamina, fortitude, deliberation, determination, peace, and compassion to crawl or walk through this journey, trusting in Him to work things out for our good, regardless of the outcome.

Everything It Takes

Remember what the Scriptures say in Romans 8:28? "And we know that all things work together for good to those who love God, to those who are the called according to His purpose."

If we believe God's Word and trust what He says, we have everything it takes to be restored when we get weak, to stand strong when all we do seems to fail, to hold on when we don't understand what's happening, and to keep trusting when we can't see the finish line.

You may be sick in your body today—life is like that; we all get sick at one time or the other. Health-wise, you may have just received the worst news of your life about yourself or someone you love. You may even be comparing your physical situation with those you've known in the past. You may have researched all the statistics concerning your situation. Or you may be keeping the bad news secret, not having talked to anyone about what you know.

Whatever else you might have done, I suggest that you make sure you do this: Turn your eyes upon Jesus, the Great I AM, and ask for His directions. If you're like me, you've never actually heard Him speak out loud, but you know in your spirit that He communicates with you in a way you can understand.

When the Healing Doesn't Come

Why does God not heal everyone who asks?

As I indicated before, I've learned not to second-guess God. Too often, in my opinion, when people are not healed, others may accuse them of not having enough faith. But that's just like saying someone is not saved enough. God has given all of us who trust Him a measure of faith. He declares that it only takes faith the size of a mustard seed to move mountainous circumstances out of your life. So faith on the part of the sick person cannot be the issue, unless they profess *no* faith in God.

It may take days or years of praying for God to heal people.

Maybe we become misled when we watch Christian TV programs that talk about healing. In one part of the program they show a film clip of people who are sick, and a few minutes later we see them well. This information can be somewhat misleading, however, because often it does not tell the lengthy journey of those who are healed. So to the person watching this program, it looks like such a miracle. I am not condemning these programs, because I thoroughly believe in what is called "faith healing." I just know from experience that people can be misled about a testimony and not realize that it may take days or years of praying for God to heal people.

I have a friend who became so disillusioned about healing that she has actually fallen away from her intense Bible study and regular attendance in church. She had prayed for both her parents to be healed, but they died. She had been constantly glued to healing programs that seemed to show God moving *right now* and healing people the very moment anyone asked Him to. It did not happen that way for her, and so it has caused her much distress.

Paul's Struggles with Illness

One of the greatest examples of God *not* healing someone is that of His powerful servant, the apostle Paul. Paul tells us in Scripture that he experienced "a thorn in the flesh" (2 Corinthians 12:7). There has been much speculation about what this thorn was, but many agree that it was some kind of ailment.

The apostle Paul definitely had the gift of healing, for we read about it in Scripture:

> Now God worked unusual miracles by the hands of Paul, so that even handkerchiefs or aprons were

> brought from his body to the sick, and the diseases left them and the evil spirits went out of them. (Acts 19:11–12)

We read in Acts 20:9–12 how Paul even raised the dead!

However, even though Paul was performing incredible miracles, God did not always answer Paul's prayers for physical healing for those around him. Paul advised Timothy, "Stop drinking only water, and use a little wine because of your stomach and your frequent illnesses" (1 Timothy 5:23, NIV). And in 2 Timothy 4:20 we read that Paul "left Trophimus sick in Miletus."

Especially significant is the fact that Paul's three prayers regarding his own "thorn in the flesh" were answered *not* with physical healing, but with a greater measure and understanding of the Lord's grace:

> Concerning this thing I pleaded with the Lord three times that it might depart from me. And He said to me, "My grace is sufficient for you, for My strength is made perfect in weakness." Therefore most gladly I will rather boast in my infirmities, that the power of Christ may rest upon me. Therefore I take pleasure in infirmities, in reproaches, in needs, in persecutions, in

> distresses, for Christ's sake. For when I am weak, then I am strong. (2 Corinthians 12:8–10)

So when you're sick and can't get well, remember what Jesus, the Great I AM, said to Paul. His grace is sufficient *for you,* and *His* strength will be made perfect in your weakness.

Physical Healing Is Not Guaranteed

It's true that Jesus took our sin and sickness on the cross with Him. It is undeniable that He is the Divine Healer. This Scripture proves it:

> He Himself bore our sins in His body on the cross, so that we might die to sin and live to righteousness; for by His wounds you were healed. (1 Peter 2:24, NASB)

Does that last statement mean that all our physical afflictions will be healed? Let's take a closer look at this passage.

One of the primary rules of biblical interpretation which must never be violated is context. What is the context in 1 Peter 2? Answer: salvation. There is no way to interpret it in any other sense. The verse is talking about Jesus dying on the cross for us, enduring our punishment and bearing our sins, thereby providing salvation for us.

When certain people get hold of this passage, however, they change the context from salvation to physical healing. Every time such people see the word *heal* in the Bible they assume it refers to the miracle of divine healing for the physical body, regardless of whether the context indicates otherwise.

But often in Scripture when healing it mentioned, it has specific reference to *spiritual* healing. There are diseases of the soul that must be healed, and the primary disease of the soul is man's unregenerate state, which is rooted in sin.

The good news is that God has provided healing for this fatal disease of the soul. And that's what Peter is talking about in 1 Peter 2:24. Peter is *not* saying that physical healing of the body is guaranteed to every believer.

Certainly, healing for the body is a benefit of Christ's death on the cross, a benefit for the church as a result of His atoning sacrifice. However, there is not—and there has never been, in the history of the church—a guarantee that God *must* heal your body. He doesn't have to!

Watch God at Work

God *does* say He will graciously entertain our prayers. He says that if we exercise faith, and if our request is in accordance with His will, He *will* hear us. But He never said that the mark of true spirituality is that you would never sneeze or sprain your ankle or get a headache.

Some within the church will try to tell you, "God's perfect will is that you are *never* going to be sick." Well, I'll tell you something: If you're honest, you'll admit that there are certain lessons you never would have learned unless the Lord flattened you out long enough to get your attention. God's plan includes teaching us things through our suffering.

So be wise. God can heal you instantly. He can use medication or health professionals as a conduit to your healing. It may take surgery or changing your diet or getting some rest or any combination of such things. Don't get so caught up in trying to hear Him that you fail to see Him working in your life through such things, or through anything else.

I can't tell you specifically *how* He works. I finally figured out that I'm not that smart. What I *can* tell you is that nothing can happen in your life that He is not aware of, and He has planned a way for you to escape the trauma and bitterness that can be caused by illness. He has promised to be with you in all things, all the way till the final consummation of the ages. He will give you peace as you ride through your storm of sickness or disease.

That's why I'm sure that I can walk through uncertain times of severe sickness...because I know the I AM.

Your Journal

Write down your answer to this question: How can your own life change as you realize more fully that the Lord is the I AM who heals you?

CHAPTER 8

I AM IS YOUR PROVIDER

And Abraham called the name of the place, The-Lord-Will-Provide; as it is said to this day, "In the Mount of the LORD it shall be provided."

GENESIS 22:14

It's amazing to me how God is concerned about everything in our lives—both big things and little things. He's just as concerned about one as He is the other.

HIS EYE IS ON THE SPARROW

I recall an occasion in the mid 1980s when I was asked to sing for the interdenominational worship service at a convention of the National Speakers Association. Zig Ziglar, the famous motivational speaker and business leader, was the guest speaker that morning. Before he got up to speak,

I noticed tears streaming down Zig's face while I was singing "His Eye Is on the Sparrow."

It's a song that asks poignant questions, and answers them as well:

Why should I feel discouraged, why should the
shadows come,
Why should my heart be lonely, and long for heaven
and home,
When Jesus is my portion? My constant friend is He:
His eye is on the sparrow, and I know He watches me.

I sing because I'm happy,
I sing because I'm free,
For His eye is on the sparrow,
And I know He watches me.

The Sermon on the Mount tells us the origin of these answers to our deepest questions. Jesus is speaking to the crowd, and He assures them of the Father's provision:

> Look at the birds of the air, for they neither sow nor reap nor gather into barns; yet your heavenly Father feeds them. Are you not of more value than they? Which of you by worrying can add

> one cubit to his stature? So why do you worry about clothing? Consider the lilies of the field, how they grow: they neither toil nor spin; and yet I say to you that even Solomon in all his glory was not arrayed like one of these. Now if God so clothes the grass of the field, which today is, and tomorrow is thrown into the oven, will He not much more clothe you, O you of little faith? (Matthew 6:26–30)

After I finished the song, Zig got up to speak, and he did so with deep emotion. He expressed that he had planned to talk about something he thought was important that morning, but as he listened to my solo, his message changed. With tear-stained eyes, but a contented look on his face, Zig stood there and spoke about his conversion experience.

He told us about Miss Jessie, who had worked for their family when Zig was growing up. Miss Jessie had spoken to young Zig again and again about Jesus Christ and how Jesus would come into your life when you asked Him and change your life forever. Miss Jessie complimented him for being a good man of high moral character, a giving man with a heart of gold, and a loving man—but she told him that all these attributes would not save his soul and get him into heaven.

Well, one day Zig finally got it, and he asked Jesus into his life. Miss Jessie was right! Zig said he had never been the same person since that day.

That morning at the speakers' convention was my first face-to-face experience with Zig Ziglar—an experience that enhanced my life and helped me gain the boldness to speak up more about Jesus' transforming power when He comes to live in our lives. Zig's testimony was not only enhancing for me, it was eye-opening for many who were listening. Some of the people expressed their desire to accept this Jesus as their own Lord and Master.

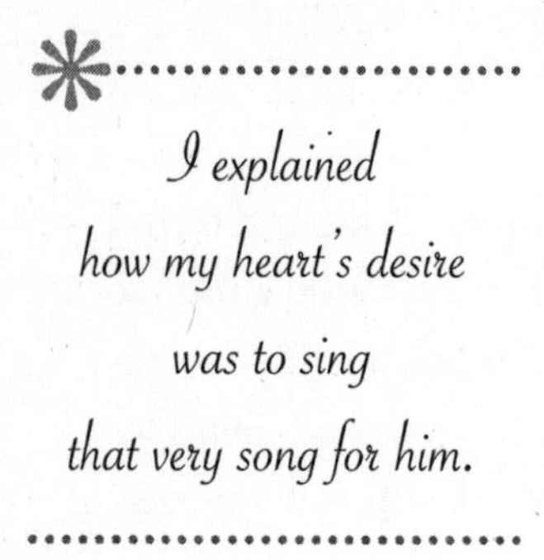

God provided several things on that fateful Sunday morning. He provided an atmosphere for Zig to give the gospel to people whose hearts had been prepared by the music. He provided Zig the opportunity to do something that he said he'd never done in that kind of environment—to witness to so many professional speakers all at one time. God provided salvation that day for those whose hearts were open to receive the best gift they could ever know.

The I AM is the Provider of all our needs, whether we see them as needs or not!

Nearly a decade later, I was fortunate to attend a Christmas gathering for the employees and contractors of the Zig Ziglar Corporation located in Plano, Texas. It was an event held every year and hosted by Zig and his beautiful wife, Jean (whom he calls "the Red Head"), and this particular year my husband, George, and I were invited.

When we were traveling to the party, I happened to say to George, "I'd love to sing 'Sweet Little Jesus Boy' for Zig tonight." End of conversation. My husband did not comment.

That evening we enjoyed some of the best food of the season, met a lot of neat people, and saw the amazing Christmas decorations in the Ziglars' home. With the party in full gear, we gathered around the stately black baby grand piano in the living room to sing Christmas carols.

While we were singing, Zig walked over to me, put his long arms around my short shoulders, leaned down to my ear, and said (in a voice like none other than Zig's), "Thelma, do you know the song 'Sweet Little Jesus Boy'?"

To which I started crying. I explained to Zig how on the way to the party, my heart's desire was to sing that very song for him. I marveled at the sensitivity of God, and remembered the Lord's promise (in Psalm 37:4) that if we delight in the Lord, He will give us the desires of our hearts. WOW! What a Provider the I AM is!

So I sang:

> *Sweet little Jesus boy,*
> *they made you be born in a manger.*
> *Sweet little holy child,*
> *didn't know who you was.*

This experience reminded me of the particular message that song had for me nearly ten years earlier, and it caused me to stop and thank God for His provision of music to help heal the souls of mankind. That night, the reminder that Jesus was sweet as a baby boy—and is still sweet as the risen Savior—rang out in the comments and sentiments of the guests there.

I was reminded that the I AM provides ways for us to remember Who He is, and how the words of songs minister so deeply to us.

Wallpaper Blessings

So many of us tend to think God is concerned only about the big problems we have or the big things we need or want. But I've learned over and over that He's concerned about *everything* that runs through our minds.

One day, on a flight to Portland, Oregon, this thought hurriedly flickered through my mind: *I'd like to have wallpaper in my house.* That's it. Just a thought. In all my years of home ownership I had never had wallpaper; we are paint lovers, as a painted surface can be washed off easily. That thought about wallpaper never entered my mind again.

I spoke that evening for the Portland Christian Center, and at the end of the meeting I noticed this lady just milling around, looking through my books, not buying one thing and looking a bit awkward. After everyone left my book table, she wandered over to me with a sweet smile on her face and a peaceful, gentle hello. Then she said, "Mrs. Wells, you really blessed me tonight, and I want to bless you. I've been a wallpaper hanger for over twenty years, and I want to come to your house in Dallas and bless you with new wallpaper."

"What? Did I hear you correctly? You want to come to my house in Dallas and hang wallpaper? How did you know I was wishing on the plane here this morning that I had wallpaper in my house?"

She said, "I didn't know, but while I was listening to you, the Lord just told me to wallpaper your house."

I laughed and cried at the same time. Again, I marveled at the mind of God who hears our every groan, care, desire, intention—all that and more—and gives us whatever He knows we need or want. That is amazing to me. I still am amazed at the Great I AM.

The rest of the wallpaper story is amazing to me also. This young woman's name was Ruth Ann. I waited two weeks before calling Ruth Ann about the wallpaper. I thought she might have been caught up in the emotions of the moment when I met her in Portland, and she may have gone home and changed her mind about coming to Dallas to work. But when I called her, she was just as excited as when we left the church laughing together. We set a date for her to come, and she informed me that she would pay her way, get a hotel, buy the paper, and give me the labor.

Now, that was just too much for me to accept. I informed her that I would pay her way, she would live in my home, I would buy my own wallpaper, and she could give the labor. After much haggling back and forth, I won.

So in July of that year, she came to my house and revitalized it.

The wallpaper itself was also an act of God. You see, I had gone to many wallpaper stores and found that the kind of wallpaper I wanted cost a small fortune. (I have high-class taste on a soda pop budget.) But only a few days before Ruth Ann was to come, I stopped by a Wallpapers To Go store, one I had visited before, and guess what. All their wallpaper was on sale, from ninety-nine cents a roll up to two dollars a roll, with nothing over that. They were going out of business at that location and had to be out of the building in only two days. So I papered seven rooms in my house for less than three hundred dollars. Look at God!

What a lesson there is in this! God not only gives us many things we desire, but He makes it convenient for us to be good stewards of what He gives us, even when we don't understand it. He is the amazing I AM of our heart's desires. WOW!

Sent by Angels

My Christmas song for Zig and my house's wallpapering were events that had no disappointment in them. However, not every desire we have is answered and provided for so quickly and easily.

My daughter Lesa and her husband, Patrick, had been married for several years and were living in an apartment in what is *not* the nicest part of town. They had been looking, without success, for a house to buy or property to build a house on. Lesa was pregnant, and they wanted to be in a new home by the time their first child was born.

As the search dragged on, they become a bit desperate and weary of looking for the right place for them to raise a family.

One day Lesa came by my office at home and asked me to go with her to look for a house. I left out the back door of my office while Lesa went out the front door. She thought

I was coming around to meet her, and I thought she was coming around to meet me. When she didn't come around, I just went back inside. On the way in, I started praying that God would lead us to the house He had picked out for Lesa and Patrick.

Why do we get surprised when God does what we ask Him to?

I stepped into my bedroom and happened to look on the bench at the foot of my bed. The newspaper was facing me with a picture of a custom-built house in an area of town they liked, and in the right price range. When Lesa eventually came back into my house to find me, I showed her the newspaper, and we agreed to go see that model home first.

On the way there, Lesa and I prayed that God would allow His ministering angels to guide us to the right place.

We followed the directions to Mockingbird Street, and two things happened. First, Lesa remembered that over three years prior, a man had told Lesa and Patrick that they would build their home in a nice community, and that they would recognize the area because their house would be on a street that started with the letter "M."

Just an aside here: I am not one to believe *everything* that someone (a prophet) says; I've got to line up what they say with the Word of God, or what they say must be a confirmation of what God has already said to me, or else I won't accept it. But at this moment, we remembered what this gentlemen had said.

The second thing to happen was this: When we turned on Mockingbird Street, there was such a sweet smell. What was especially strange about the smell is that there happened to be a horse stable on the left side of the street, and I have certainly never smelled sweetness coming from a horse stable before. (You know what I mean, don't you?)

This sweet smell continued as we stopped and parked and went inside the model home.

Now remember, we had prayed for angels to direct us to the house God prepared for Lesa and Patrick. As we entered the model home, standing in the spacious living room was a lady with the kindest, most inviting smile on her face. She said, "Hello ladies. The angels sent you here."

Both Lesa and I were astonished! (Why do people get surprised when God does what they ask Him to?)

I asked the lady why she said that. Her reply was, "I was just sitting here praying and asking God to have His angels bring the next person into this home. You see, I own the development, and I've asked God to fill these homes with people who love the Lord. I believe that God uses His angels to work for us. So, I believe He sent you in."

By this time Lesa is in tears, I'm grinning like a Cheshire cat, and Fern Barnett, the owner of Fern Heights Housing

Addition, is inviting us back to her desk with the biggest smile on her face I'd seen in a long time. I explained to her how Lesa and I had prayed on the way there that God would use His angels to direct us to the place where she and Patrick should live. And now, we had found it! Lesa, Fern, and I became friends instantly.

God Comes Through

But that's not all. Patrick had wanted to build on a corner lot on a hill. Would you believe there was only one corner lot left in the development, and it was on a hill with an adjacent lot? Lesa and Patrick agreed to buy both of the lots at a discount, because this development was ninety-nine percent completed.

So the process for purchasing the land on which to build their house got underway. There was more drama to come.

You see, I love Patrick and Lesa, but Lesa (at that time) had a viewpoint I couldn't share. She had a wait-and-see attitude: *Wait and see if this is God speaking to us and providing these lots, or whether it's only our emotions making us want this.* Patrick was ready, but Lesa was cautiously praying—while personally, I was fuming because hadn't God already spoken when that angel conversation was going on? What more did Lesa want?

Fern had told us that there was another lady who said she wanted that property and who was still trying to get the down payment. So I could not understand Lesa's reasoning and her delay. For two days I called Lesa, telling her to get her buns out there and sign that contract before somebody else did.

Here's the real drama. On the third day, Lesa woke up before daylight with urgency in her spirit. She woke up Patrick and told him to get up—they were going right then to sign the contract.

They drove out to the model home office and got there at eight o'clock, even though Fern normally did not arrive until ten or eleven. Would you believe that on that morning Fern got there before nine o'clock, saying she just decided to get there early that day?

Lesa and Pat bought the lot and signed the contract. As they were walking out of the office, the other lady who had wanted the property walked in with her money ready to purchase. But she was too late. The I AM had done His work, and He proved that when He provides for us, even if we respond slowly and we pause for reassurance, His will for us will be done.

So the property was purchased and the house was built.

But there's more drama still. My husband and I had promised to give Lesa and Patrick the closing costs when the house was built and ready to occupy. At the time we promised this, we had the money they would need. But later we got a big notice from our Uncle Sam to pay some taxes we had not anticipated. When we paid those taxes, there was little left for our children.

One of the standards we have in our family is to not promise anything we know or think we cannot do. So there was no reason for Lesa and Patrick to think we could not keep our commitment.

As the house was being finished and the closing time drew near, I had no choice but to break the news to them that we had no money to pay for their closing. That was hard to disclose. But when I told Lesa, she just sat up in the bed and told me not to worry; God would provide what they needed, because He had opened the way for them to get this far, and He would come through for them again.

I did not see any possibility of that money coming in for the closing. Oh, me of questionable faith!

The next day after I told this to Lesa, she came to me and said, "Mama, you don't need to feel bad about not having the money. God showed me in a dream this morning that everything was fine."

She explained her dream. "You know the great room as you walk into the house? There's a column there. In my dream there's a big eight-foot angel standing in our house. The angel is transparent except for the bright white outline all around him. His hair is in a pageboy cut, and he's standing in the house, looking around with approval on his face.

Surrounding him are little baby angels just flying and playing and having a good time—they're happy!"

Then Lesa said, "Mama, God still has angels watching over this house and the money. Don't worry."

My confidence level increased through the faith of my daughter and the word of the testimony in her dream. I started believing what my great-grandmother used to say all the time: "Baby, God will make a way!"

The date came for the closing, and there was absolutely no money from anywhere for the closing costs. It was a Friday. But the builder called Lesa that day and told her that they couldn't close that day after all because the final inspection had not been done. Lesa was fine with that, and I was as nervous as a cat on a hot tin roof. I guess my faith was not as set in concrete as I'd thought. I just could not see where the money was coming from, but Lesa was confident things would work out.

The following Monday morning, I opened the mail and there was an unexpected check for more than the amount of the closing costs. While I was phoning my husband to tell him to come get this check and deposit it in the bank, I was shouting, "Praise God! He really is a provider!"

I knew that if we got the check to the bank before three o'clock that afternoon, we would be in good shape to give the gift we had promised.

Would you believe the builder called Lesa and Patrick that same morning and set the closing for three o'clock that afternoon? My husband and I were able to go to the bank, fill out the gift papers, and get the money needed to give our children. God kept His promise to provide our needs according to His riches in glory through Christ Jesus. My husband and I were able to keep our promise—but without the great Provider keeping *His* promise, we had no way of keeping ours.

The Proven Provider

Yes, God is *Jehovah Jireh*—our provider (Genesis 22:14), and He has proven Himself to keep His promises of provision in every situation.

If you have not set your needs before God, you may be missing out on the great provisions God has planned for you before the foundation of the world.

Trust Him. Try Him. Prove Him. Honor Him with your trust. When there's an urgent need, and you ask in faith, believing Him—He will never let you down.

Your Journal

Write down your answer to this question: How can your own life change as you realize more deeply that the Lord I AM is in every way your Provider?

CHAPTER 9

I AM IS YOUR BANNER

And Moses built an altar and called its name,
The-LORD-Is-My-Banner.
EXODUS 17:15

From my home away from home—DFW International Airport—I called my sister one day. I heard panic in her voice when she answered the telephone.

"How are you doing?" I asked.

To which she answered, "Girl, not good. I just saw a mouse run across my floor like he was paying rent here. He walked between my legs—and I'm not doing well with that."

What I wanted to know was, "Are you still in the room with it? Why are you not up on the roof?"

She said it caught her by surprise and she was stunned. She hadn't seen a mouse since she moved to that apartment years ago. Now she was on her way to the rental office to report this intrusion and to tell them to send in troops, the militia, the National Guard, or whomever. Just get that unwanted mouse out of her apartment!

This was the first time I realized she and I have the same fear or dislike (or panic) when we encounter any mouse or r_t (I don't even like to say the name). In fact, the most fear I have ever experienced in my life was at the sight of a certain r_t. I believe these rodents are the only varmint that could actually give me a heart attack. I hate them! I'm terrified of them! I don't even consider it funny when someone tries to play with me with a stuffed one.

Ask a few of my best friends how I feel about that.

One day we were sitting in an arena during a Women of Faith conference when a mouse fell from a ceiling rafter and hit Marilyn Meberg's shoe with tremendous velocity. Sheila Walsh saw it and squealed. Patsy Clairmont curled her legs in her chair. Luci Swindoll laughed. And I picked up my purse and held it in my lap for the rest of the conference while stretching my legs straight out for as long as I could hold them there. That was a sight to see!

The ordeal was so unnerving that I had to really pray for strength and for God to remove my fear of r_ts. I'd become paralyzed by the fear of something which, to most people, would only bring the response, "They're more afraid of you than you are of them." Don't matter! I still don't like them.

However, as I honestly faced up to my past reactions to any mouse or r_t, I knew I needed either therapy or the Lord to deliver me from this fear.

I'm happy to say that I have not had the opportunity to test whether I'm delivered or not, and I hope I won't. But I can say that I've asked God to help me deal with such a creature without panicking, if an encounter with one of them occurs again.

Worse Fears

There have been more urgent occurrences in my life that caused me fear—situations much worse than dealing with mice dropping from the ceiling. These experiences were no joking matter.

As a small child, I did not realize the kind of danger I lived in every day as a black girl in the South where prejudice was the order of the day. All I knew was that I could not go places I wanted to go because I was restricted on account of my skin color. I knew there were signs on the downtown water fountains that said "Colored" and "White." I also knew that the "White" water interested me more than the "Colored," and occasionally I would slip and drink from the "White" water fountain. I know now that I could have gotten in a lot of trouble for disobeying the law.

Much later, fear was the last thing on my mind when I went inside the doors of a secretarial school in my hometown and was bodily thrown out on the street after being refused the right to register for school. When this happened, all I felt was anger, sadness, embarrassment, and disappointment. (Earlier, when I'd called the school to see if they were registering, the person on the other end of the telephone answered yes and invited me to come down to enroll.)

I started fantasizing about what I would do if it happened again.

When I eventually went to a four-year university (where I would earn a bachelor's degree), I had no idea that for two semesters one of the teachers would ignore calling my name from her roll and refuse to call on me to participate in class because, as she put it, "I've never taught a Negress before and I don't intend to now." (She really was a good teacher, though.)

FEARFUL EVER AFTER?

In a deeper way, I had never tasted real grief that was traumatic and fearful to me until I got married. (So much for "And they lived happily ever after.") Actually, the incident that messed up my mind this way was not all that bad—but I thought it was.

I entered marriage with the assumption that the man I married was everything I would ever need in my whole life. I thought he would be my knight in shining armor, attending to my every whim, and totally devoted to me and to nothing else, and I planned to be the very same to him. (I had it bad!)

Soon after we were married, I began to get an inkling that I might have misjudged this situation. Especially when one day my husband, while talking with a friend who was visiting, asked me to come turn on a lamp that was within arm's reach of him. When I asked *him* to please turn on the lamp, since he was sitting next to it, he replied, "When I tell you to do something, I mean do it *now.*"

Oh nooooo!

I was not as anointed in the Word then as I am now. So I told him where to take his arm and that lamp and what to do with them when he got there. (I was not nice.)

He must have been trying to show off in front of his friend. It didn't work!

The good that came out of this is that in well over forty years since that day, my husband has never again tried to be that demanding.

At the time, however, this occasion caused me more trauma than I had ever experienced with someone I loved and adored. I grew up with love and respect in our home as the order of the day. So when this incident happened with my new husband, I wondered if I had made a mistake. I wondered if things like this were going to be a part of my life from then on. I pondered if I'd done something to make him speak to me that way. I questioned if this was just what married people did, and if I should have done what he asked without defiance.

The incident frightened me enough that I started fantasizing about what I would do if it happened again. I remembered when I lived in a housing project in Dallas where the lady next door would literally fight with her husband every weekend. Sometimes they would send each other to the hospital. Was that my future?

Every time my husband and I would have a disagreement, I got more and more paranoid. He never talked ugly to me again, and he never disrespected me again, but that first disappointment took me to a place of mentally replaying that first tape over and over again. Each time I would play it, I think it got noisier and noisier, creating a lot of static in my insecure brain.

Things did not get better in my mind. I tried to not speak my opinion for fear it would turn him away from me. I tried to do everything right for fear he would be disgusted with me. I tried not to sound argumentative because I did not want to anger him. Okay, I was a mess!

But my mind was playing games with me like I don't know what.

After nearly five years of pretending to be someone I was not for fear of rejection, my feelings caught up with me, and I experienced what I call situational depression. For two and a half years I battled with low self-worth, overeating, crying, fainting spells, and fits of anger. Why? Because of my self-inflicted fear.

Getting Rid of the Monsters

I was taught all my life that God will protect your heart, mind, and body, and that you don't need to be afraid of anything. The most beautiful portrait of this teaching was when I was about five or six years old.

I used to have nightmares about monsters coming in the house and seeing monster faces through the front door's four-pane window at our back-alley apartment in Dallas. I would scream and cry and run to my great-grandfather for protection. He always comforted me and made the monsters go away.

But one day was extra special.

When I saw the monsters, Daddy Harrell, my great-grandfather, asked me to lie down on the roll-away bed he and my great-grandmother had on the screened front porch. I trusted this old man because he had been my father figure for as long as I could remember, and there was nobody in the world kinder to me than he was.

He asked me if I wanted to get rid of the monsters forever so they would never bother me again.

My answer was, “Yes sir.”

Then he said, “Pooch (that’s what he called me), do you trust me?”

“Yes sir.”

“Then close your eyes and recite the Lord’s Prayer and the Twenty-third Psalm, one after the other, until you are not scared anymore. You got it? The Lord’s Prayer and the Twenty-third Psalm.” He had taught me this prayer and this Scripture when we played church.

So I followed his instructions. I did just what he told me to do. I don’t know how many times I repeated them, but I do know this: When I felt completely relieved, I opened my eyes, and what did I see in the sky above? The soft, cotton-like, billowing clouds had rolled together and formed a head-and-shoulder outline of Jesus as seen in His most popular portrait. His hair was long and wavy. His eyes were soft and kind. He wore a white flowing robe on His shoulders. I knew who He was.

I’ve never feared monsters or much else again. Hallelujah! My great-granddad taught me who to go to for total protection in time of fear.

Why didn't I remember that right away after I got married? How easily we forget that we cannot protect ourselves completely. But God can! After all, He is the Great I AM. He is our Banner (as Scripture says), which tells us that He is our Protector.

A Banner for the Battle

Since recovering from my bout with situational depression (and my marriage is now as happy as it can be), I have practiced calling on God at the first sign of fear. I've finally learned that the Great I AM is my Banner who goes before me, stands beside me, and shields me from evil and danger in every situation.

What does it really mean to say that the Great I AM is my Banner?

We are all in a constant battle in this world over time, money, family, church, health, or whatever area you're battling in. And that's what fear is...a battle. In a battle or a time of war, a banner is highly significant.

In the old days, banners were an important part of warfare. They became a rallying point, an encouragement, a reminder. Any good general knew the need for such encouragement, so commanding officers always placed their banners in strategic positions. It was a beautiful sight, as everyone knew. In fact, in Scripture we find the phrase "awesome as an army with banners" as a compliment recognizing beauty (in Song of Solomon 6:4 and 6:10).

A banner is a logo, a flag, a sail, a signal, and a token. It was to be conspicuous. In a time of rejoicing over salvation, David says this: "In the name of our God we will set up our banners!" (Psalm 20:5). And in another psalm, David praised the Lord with these words: "You have raised a banner for those who fear you—a rallying point in the face of attack" (Psalm 60:4, NLT).

I've learned to wrap myself up in His banner and to stay in the warm protection of His promise.

So the banner becomes the identification for the person needing encouragement, protection, and care. This banner should be put in a strategically prominent place to be seen by all. It's to show off (if you will) as a display of the protection that shields whoever is involved in the battle.

That's why, after a victory for the people of God in a battle against the Amalekites, Moses built an altar and called it *Jehovah Nissi*, "The-LORD-Is-My-Banner" (Exodus 17:15).

With this truth in mind—that the Great I AM is our Banner—I can pray in this way: "Lord, You have given a flag of assurance to all of us, whether a child afraid of an imaginary monster, or any person being discriminated against, or ignored, or having a dark closet experience. You have already seen where we are, where we're going, and when we'll get there."

God has seen the "movie" of our life before it was filmed, and He has gone before us to light the way and set our feet in the right path. Our history will prove that God has been trying to get us to see His protective covering all the time.

But so often we just won't pay attention to it. We get our annual checkup with the doctor and are afraid that the doctor will discover something we don't want. Or we fear we'll lose our job. Or we fear something will happen to harm those we love most, or that something else will hurt these relationships.

Whatever it is, the I AM your Banner has already been there and taken care of the situation. Whether you get what you prayed for or not, God is still waving His banner of protection over your situation. Nothing slips up on Him or catches Him by surprise.

Sometimes in my neighborhood we sing, "Don't wait till the battle is over to shout now!" That's right. And God said He has already paved the way for us to win the war even if you lose the battle.

I've learned to wrap myself up in His banner and to stay in the warm protection of His promise. I've learned that "God has not given us a spirit of fear, but of power and of love and of a sound mind" (2 Timothy 1:7).

A Supernatural Battle

I've seen the Great I AM perform modern-day miracles using His righteous banner.

Someone very dear to me was incarcerated and was about to be killed because some of the inmates thought he had snitched on them. The plot was about to be carried out one night when I got the urge to make a telephone call to the chaplain for the prison, to tell him that something did not seem right.

At the same instant the inmates were about to injure this prisoner, a guard asked him to come out because someone wanted to see him. (This was late in the evening after visiting hours were over, and most people were in bed.) It was the chaplain—he had the urge to visit this prisoner before morning. He arrived in the nick of time. The person was moved away from danger, seemingly out of the clear blue sky.

I know what really happened in the supernatural. God already had a plan for this situation. He used me to call the chaplain, who followed the dictates of his spirit and went to the prison. The person was saved from being hurt because the banner of God, *Jehovah Nissi,* had already gone before him to let him know who cares. That battle was already won because the prayers of the righteous availed much.

As you are cast into the prison cells of life, having nowhere to go, no fresh air to breathe, no "White" water to drink, where monsters seem to be all around you—put this picture in your mind: a huge portrait of God, looking like He does in Michelangelo's rendition of the Christ. And there's something added to the scene—a bright, beautiful, waving red flag with big white letters on it that spell, *I AM the Lord your Banner.*

Yes, I have learned that *I can* because I know that I know the I AM. And even when the day comes that I see another mouse or r_t, I will know God has gone before me and has taken care of even that!

The Fear Moses Knew

Have you thought about how many occasions Moses had to be fearful?

Let's just start with the burning bush. How would *you* feel if you walked up to a bush that was burning, and you could not smell the smoke, and it was not turning black or withering—and furthermore it started *talking* to you? You'd be shaking in your sandals! This voice tells you to take those sandals off and walk up to it. Without God's help, you'd be running for cover.

Then the voice from the bush (God) tells you to go back to the place which you ran away from long ago because you killed somebody there. It doesn't matter that the murder happened forty years ago; somebody who knew about it might still be living. I bet *you* would try to make excuses too, just like Moses did.

When Moses told God what He already knew—that he could not talk good—God had already gone before him and planted Moses' brother Aaron to speak for him. The I AM had gone before him.

Then when Moses was on his way to talk to Pharaoh, God told Moses He was going to kill him (read about it in Exodus 4:24–26). Now, you let God tell you He's going to kill you, and see if you're not scared! That must have been confusing to Moses, because God had just told him to go back to Egypt, and now here God was, talking about killing him. What's up with that?

But God had gone before Moses and had placed into the mind of Zipporah, Moses' wife, the reason for God's anger with her husband. She immediately carried out the mandate to circumcise their sons. The Jewish law had commanded this to be done on the eighth day of a male child's birth, but Moses had not done this. Moses' life was saved because the I AM had gone before him and prepared his once-pagan wife to understand and solve the problem.

There were a number of other experiences that must have frightened Moses.

One of them was his battle with the Amalekites, the account of which is where we find that term *Jehovah Nissi* (in Exodus 17:15). It was after Moses defeated the Amalekites (who were a type of Satan, and a kingdom of darkness) that he made the altar and called it *Jehovah Nissi,* which means "The LORD is my banner" or "The I AM is my banner."

Every day you and I are in either an emotional, physical, or spiritual battle, fighting Satan and his cohorts. But be of good cheer. God has overcome the evils of this world! Through the death and resurrection of His Son, all the powers of darkness are defeated; Christ has "disarmed principalities and powers," and He "made a public spectacle of them, triumphing over them" in the cross (Colossians 2:15).

All his life, Moses was surrounded by trouble. He had a lot to be afraid of. But he knew he had the I AM as his Banner going before him. He and the children of Israel were hemmed in with the Red Sea ahead of them and Pharaoh's army behind them. They went on to experience forty years of wandering and backtracking in the wilderness with no earthly sign of enough food and water to ensure the survival of so vast a multitude. Plus the people were forever bickering and challenging Moses' authority.

It's obvious Moses had a lot of scary times while carrying out his assignment to free his people. But through it all, he was keenly aware that God, the Great I AM, was the Banner who went before him to protect him in all his ways.

This same God, the Great I AM, goes before *you*—so you need not be afraid about anything that happens in your life. The Great I AM is your *Jehovah Nissi*; the Great I AM is your Banner.

Your Journal

Write down your answer to this question: How can your own life change as you understand better how the Lord is your Banner?

CHAPTER 10

THE POWER CONNECTION

Without Me you can do nothing.

JOHN 15:5

When I was doing training seminars for various corporations, organizations, and other groups, I liked to start with a mental exercise to help everyone wake up and get their adrenaline pumping. One of my favorites was a puzzle called "The Nine Dots." The object of this exercise was to start from any point and draw exactly four connecting lines (without lifting your pen) so that each of the nine dots has at least one line running through it.

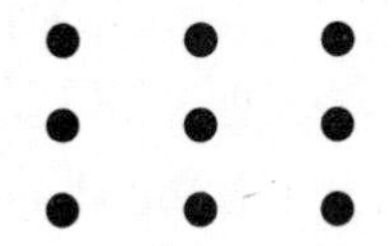

Before each session I would practice trying to do this, but without success. I don't know why this was so difficult for me to do, try after try after try. Of course I had a copy of the answer, and in the session itself I would refer to this pattern and trace the correct answer on the board or flip chart, so the participants never knew I had such a hard time getting it right. It was so simple when I looked at the guide—but so difficult when I tried to get it on my own.

Try it. See if you can get it.

The very first time I attempted to connect those dots, I was altogether off base and got a headache trying to connect them. I assumed I had to stay inside the square of dots while connecting them with only four lines. It didn't occur to me that my assumption was erroneous. No one *said* I had to stay within the dots. But my controlled way of thinking didn't want me to venture in any direction beyond my mental conditioning; I was powerless to connect those dots because of my lack of adventure, my lack of vision outside the dots.

God Does It Different

As people who think we know how to do most things well, we find ourselves attempting to put God inside a box, because we think we've figured out how to connect with Him through our own intellect and our own conditioning. Because we read or study His Word, attend church, work in ministries, act holy, talk about "our God," conduct Bible studies, attend Christian conferences, teach our families about God, and "perform" for Him—we assume we really know Him and understand how He works in our lives.

Have you ever thought you knew how God was going to work for you, and banked your life on it, only to discover that He went in a different direction? We are told by many Christian preachers, teachers, authors, etc., that if we do *this,* God will do *that.* For the most part, they're telling the truth, if they predicate what they say on the promises of God. God cannot lie or go back on His Word. The problem with what these communicators say is that they (and we) make it seem like God will do this immediately and automatically whenever we ask.

Okay, I'm going to get technical with you now. When God fulfills His promise to you, He does this not *when* you ask, but *before* you ask, because there's no time with God. He has straightened out your situation *before the foundation of the world!* But when you can't see it happening before your eyes...when you give Him a timeframe and He does not do what you asked...when it seems that He has not heard you or certainly has not shown you that He has...that's when you get impatient, and you worry, fret, cry, and begin to lose hope.

I believe if we could see the entire process from someone's first prayer request all the way to their glad and grateful testimony about what God did, we would understand to a greater depth this concept of God answering prayer. However, the process is different for each situation, and it's always controlled by the sovereign God of the universe. God does not work within our concept of how things should be; He is *not* a nine-dot Person. He is the Knower, Maker, and Giver of every good and perfect gift. He operates under His own authority and is not limited to what we think, or to our feeble conditioning. Hallelujah! He doesn't order our lives as though it's a game of intellect or wit. No, He shows us step by step how to live according to His precepts and examples.

Staying Connected

In order to live our lives in this step-by-step way with the Lord, what we have to do is *abide* in Him.

Jesus clearly states this:

> Abide in Me, and I in you. As the branch cannot bear fruit of itself, unless it abides in the vine, neither can you, unless you abide in Me. I am the vine, you are the branches. He who abides in Me, and I in him, bears much fruit; for without Me you can do nothing. (John 15:4–5)

Then He speaks these words:

> If you abide in Me, and My words abide in you, you will ask what you desire, and it shall be done for you. (John 15:7)

When you read these Scriptures, what do they say to you?

And what does "abide" really mean, after all?

Okay, let's see. Various dictionaries express the meaning in these ways: "to remain in a place"; "to stay"; "to rest or dwell"; "to continue permanently"; "to continue to be sure or firm"; "to endure"; "to wait patiently for"; "to dwell or sojourn." (You may not have wanted all that information, but it's essential that we understand the richness of what this word encompasses so that we can understand and live out this concept of *abiding*.)

We trust the power source to give us the energy we need to produce what we expect.

In John 15, to "abide" is to stay in harmony and obedience to God; to stay connected to the power source for our lives and well-being; and to be in the right position to get the blessings, answers, guidance, and liberties He has provided for us even before we were born.

One of our problems with God's connections for us is that we go around trying to connect the dots in our lives without seeking the Dot Controller, the Holy Spirit. We try to put God in a box and make Him be what we think He should be. We take other people's word for what He ought to be or may be, but fail to look outside the comfort zone of our own experiences and see the reality outside ourselves. How arrogant of us! Who appointed us god?

The truth is that we have no power without Him working in us. The power is in the vine, the Lord Almighty. His people are the branches: "I am the vine," He said; "you are the branches." And He added, "He who abides in Me, and I in him, bears much fruit; for without Me you can do nothing." Our connection to Him is the power source to the promise of abundant living as promised to those who belong to Him: "I have come that they may have life, and have it to the full" (John 10:10, NIV).

If you are connected to the power source, you have full power to ask God for what you need, and you can expect it. We cannot see or hear any power flowing from an electrical outlet, and on our own we can't sense that any power is there unless we get shocked by the electric current. We *believe,* however, that if the electric bill is paid and the power lines are working, that when we plug in our computers or appliances, they will work. We trust the power source to give us the energy we need to produce what we expect.

God is so much bigger than any electric current. He is the Creator of the current!

And God is also much bigger than our appliances or computers. He created the intelligence to invent computers.

God is likewise so much bigger than our questions and events. He completely understands what's going on with us. He is the only power that can confuse the enemy when he attacks, rebuke the devourer when he thinks he's won the battle for our souls, combat the vicious attacks of spiritual warfare when our families are falling apart, turn around our children when they are going down the wrong road, provide for our needs when we can't see our way, heal our bodies when they are sick, offer true forgiveness when we sin, give us hope in despair, comfort us when we grieve, bear our burdens when the load gets too heavy, open closed doors, close doors we don't need to walk through, speak peace in our hearts and minds when there seems to be no peace, guide us when we need to make decisions, listen to us when nobody else cares, give us the desire of our hearts...do you get the picture? Nobody but God can do all this and more!

We have the plug...God has the power.

So you don't have to rack your brain trying to connect the dots. The dots have been connected for you in the words of the Holy Bible. From Genesis (the beginning of time as we know it) all the way through to the maps, God in His Word is showing His power through His *love* for mankind.

In the beginning He created us in love. In the closing chapter, in the Book of Revelation, He ends the ages with His redeeming love. And in between, throughout all sixty-six books, He demonstrates His love. His power is represented by His overwhelming, amazing, unparalleled *love* for you and me. God's name and nature are LOVE. Glory to His name!

So, don't stress yourself out trying to second-guess God. Plug into His power source and rely on Him to connect the dots in your life.

God Has the Solution

The answer to "The Nine Dots" brainteaser is simple when you study how it's done. You've got to go outside the square and risk what's outside the square to connect the dots in this game.

But God does not play games. His directions are not risky. They don't challenge you to try and figure them out. He just wants us to abide (stay connected, live by His words, be obedient to His commands) *in Him* and let Him do His perfect will in our lives. No game...just fact!

I'll show you the solution to "The Nine Dots" at the end of this chapter. *God* will show you the solution to your circumstances. Just ask Him, trust Him, listen to Him, seek Him, obey Him, and be persistent to do His will. Allow His Spirit to show you the solution. Take God out of the box. He is the Omnipotent One, the Omniscient One, and the Omnipresent One. In other words, He's God all by Himself. He don't need nobody else!

THE WAY, THE TRUTH, THE LIFE

Remember what Jesus said in John 14:6—He is the Way, the Truth, and the Life, and no one comes to the Father except by Him.

Jesus is the Way.

In the long-ago days of Abraham, God defined for us how "to keep the way of the LORD": It's "by doing what is right and just" (Genesis 18:19, NIV). The Way of the Lord is doing what is right and just, and only Jesus makes this possible.

Jesus is also the Truth. *"I tell you the truth,"* He says, "before Abraham was born, *I am!*" (John 8:58, NIV). For us, the Truth of the Lord is *believing* in Him. He is the truth from start to finish, because Jesus also says,

> I am the Alpha and the Omega, the Beginning and the End, the First and the Last. (Revelation 22:13)

Jesus is also the Life, for He is the Creator of Life:

> For by him all things were created: things in heaven and on earth, visible and invisible, whether thrones or powers or rulers or authorities; all things were created by him and for him. He is before all things, and in him all things hold together. (Colossians 1:16–17, NIV)

And for us, the Life of the Lord is His Spirit living in us.

Do you think you can connect with Jesus who has shown you the facts about who He is? Do you think His power is *greater than anything else in this world*? Can you trust Him enough to allow Him to connect the dots in your life? If so, don't stress over the solution. It's already given to you. Just trace it and see how accurate you will be! It's all solved for you.

Here is the solution to "The Nine Dot Puzzle":

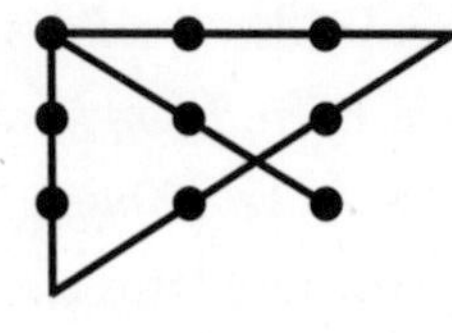

Your Journal

Write down your answer to this question: How can your own life change as you live out the fact that the Lord is your power connection?

CHAPTER 11

OBEDIENCE REALLY IS BETTER

Behold, to obey is better than sacrifice.

1 SAMUEL 15:22

Bobby was the sweetest little boy, with beautiful, dreamy brown eyes, a smile that could charm anybody, a spirit so generous that he would give you the shirt off his back. His sense of humor caused him to be the entertainment at any gathering. People loved being around him and listening to him talk. He had a passionate love for his family, and you could not find a better friend.

There were a number of boys around Bobby's age in the neighborhood where he grew up. (Maybe that was both a blessing and a curse.) These boys did everything together. They loved to fish, play at the neighborhood park, swim, and do boy things—always together.

Bobby was also exposed to the finer things in life like the arts, the symphony, Christian retreats and camps, sports, travel, good books, uplifting television programs, and church. His mother and father were supportive of his desires to play sports, pursue music, and learn to swim and all of his various activities in and out of school. The kid had it good.

Late one evening, after Bobby had been at the local park, his mother noticed a strange look in his eyes. Bobby was talking with a slur and walking like he was floating.

Oh no! Was this what his parents had been warned about? Were these the kind of danger signals that parents are told to watch for? Could it be that their precious Bobby was doing drugs?

Prison and Worse

Bobby's mother went into hysterics. She interrogated Bobby but got an answer she believed to be a lie. He said he had not done drugs. But his actions and the odor on his clothes told a different story.

Looking back, the parents recognized that other danger signs had been there. The slide in his grades for his school work that semester, plus his waning interest in anything except going to the park with his friends, were the tell-tale evidence that Bobby's parents, like so many other parents, often ignored. They'd rather not know the truth. But the truth in this situation was bound to come out.

Bobby's drug use grew into a full-blown addiction, causing many hospitalizations, drug treatments, and eventually separation from his family for a long period of time in one of the places where addicts ultimately end up—prison. In spite of the fact that Bobby accepted Christ at an early age and had rededicated himself to Christ after accepting the call to preach and become an ambassador for Christ, he chose the life of torment and trauma that drugs and other addictions cause.

Why did he go down this path of virtual hell?

The only person who could have changed the course of his life was Bobby himself. He had lived a life of disobedience to God, had ignored the warnings of God, and had thrown caution to the wind. He had willfully disobeyed his parents, the law, and the unction of the Holy Spirit living inside him.

The possible consequences he faced included not only incarceration, but either death or being maimed or debilitated, with permanent physical and mental damage to his body and mind. Furthermore, the continuance of drug use would likely cause him to become alienated from his family and friends. This possibility seemed worst of all, because Bobby loved his family.

Bobby's story reminds me of the story of the prodigal son who went away from a wonderful home—where he had power and prestige—to follow a life of selfish pleasure and all the sins that go hand-in-hand with that. This young man did not end up in a prison institution; he ended up in a prison of hog slop, poverty, shame, guilt, embarrassment, and disillusionment. You see, he thought he had the right answers when he first left home. Partying, gambling, chasing women, drinking, being his own man, and learning about the world were so exciting. But when his money was gone, his friends left too. They left without paying him back for all the times he told them, "Drinks for everybody are on me." Now he could not buy the ladies any more presents.

After his clothes were taken off his back and he ended up eating slop with pigs, this young man had two choices (as I see it): One, he could have been stupid or frightened enough to tell himself he could never again go back home because his father was too angry with him to accept him back. Or two, he could have swallowed his pride, admitted his sin, and gone back home with a humble spirit to accept the consequences. This guy got smart and regained his senses in the hog pen, and chose number two. And you know what happened next (if you've read Luke 15).

Why Do We Disobey?

What makes us disobedient? Why is it that you don't have to teach a child to do bad things, but they do them automatically?

The reason is that we were born in sin and sharpened in iniquity. When Adam and Eve fell in the Garden of Eden, sin came into the world. Immediately Adam and Eve's DNA was altered, and they began to produce a sin nature in all their descendents (you and me).

The world into which we were all born is a fallen place. The iniquities of our ancestors flow through our bloodstream. (I hate that!) Each of us is susceptible to disobeying God—it's called SIN. (I *really* hate that—but it's true.)

Maybe you have never been in jail or eaten from a pig trough, but you've been a prisoner to something else. You have eaten the bitter recipe that sin prepares for us all. Every action has a reaction, and every sin has a consequence. As my great-grandmother used to say, "Every dog has his day." (No, I don't know what it means either; it just sounded appropriate right here in this context.) We sin because sin can be attractive; it just looks like fun. We sin because we give in to temptations. Encountering the temptation is not sin; yielding to it is.

We sin to try to make ourselves look good. For example, we abuse our credit cards to purchase things we don't need and may not even like, just to impress other people (who really don't care). We sin because we want to be accepted by other people. We will join an organization or go places or say things that we know are not acceptable to us, doing it out of our need for association.

My great-grandmother had a mini-sermon for everything. She taught me, "Be nice to everybody, but *pick* your friends and associates. If they are doing things you know are wrong, get out of their company. When you do right, you will often stand alone, by yourself. But stand there. It's better to stand up for good than to fall down for bad. It's hard getting up again."

Getting Free

Bobby and the prodigal discovered that truth. Bobby now speaks to his family with words of wisdom and truth. The real story will be told when he is free and back on his own.

Very few people get completely over an addiction by going to counseling and drug treatment programs. The only people who remain completely free are those who surrender their addictions, and everything else, to the deliverance that only God Almighty can give. If God delivers them, they have no thoughts or desires to walk down that road again. If they were to say they are still an addict, they would not be telling the truth.

As Jesus said, "If the Son makes you free, you shall be free indeed" (John 8:36). Being "free indeed" means they do not have the right to label themselves as still being the way they were—because now they are truly new creatures in Christ Jesus.

Anytime you make up your mind to do right, evil is lurking around the corner to try and make a liar out of you. The enemy of your soul is seeking to devour you. Nobody can deny that when they want to follow the right path, the tempter is there to show you a different way. He's so shrewd that he can strike the smartest person, the coolest dude, the most intelligent business person, the most controlled lady, the most powerful preacher, the most astute leader, the most loyal spouse, the highest government official, the noblest head in academia, and the most talented athlete, actor, musician, or professional person you know. In other words, nobody's exempt.

The only people who remain completely free are those who surrender their addictions, and everything else, to the deliverance that only God Almighty can give.

Jesus warned us: "The thief comes only to steal and kill and destroy" (John 10:10, NIV). That word *kill* is so final. When you kill something, it does not live again. Kill a bug and see what happens. Kill a bird and it will not fly again. Kill a bee and it will not pollinate the flowers.

Just so, the thief (Satan) comes to take life away from us that God has already designed for us. The thief kills us by tempting us with things that are ungodly. He camouflages our temptations with what we like to hear and what he knows will motivate us.

This is just like he did with Eve in the Garden of Eden—he told her what he knew would motivate her: "For God knows that in the day you eat of it your eyes will be opened, and you will be like God, knowing good and evil" (Genesis 3:5). That lowdown thief tempted her pride and got her confused about what God had told her, and she slid down the road of sin because of a lie.

Every sinful temptation we get is a lie from Satan. What Eve heard from him was too good to be true. She had already heard the truth and was content with it until the master liar spoke and woke up her desire for more knowledge and control.

Eventually her eyes were opened, all right. She found out she was clothes-less, and she got embarrassed and tried to hide. Her husband ate the fruit after she did, and he tried to cover up his sin by playing the blame game. It didn't work. God confronted them both, and there was no hiding place.

That's what Bobby and the prodigal found out as well: There's no hiding place. Your sins will find you out!

YOUNG EXAMPLES OF OBEDIENCE

Now let me tell you about four other boys who have blown me away with their respect and determination to be obedient regardless of what it costs them. These boys were teenagers, very young men who apparently picked friends who shared their same goals, aspirations, and faith. They, like Bobby and the prodigal, were trained in their faith and witnessed high standards and loyalty to what is true and good in their homes and community. But these four boys also had surrendered wholeheartedly to the God of creation. They had determined in their hearts that they would have no other gods before the Sovereign God of the universe. They had made up their minds to not betray the God of their forefathers.

These four young men—prime examples of the value of strict obedience to God—are written about in the book of Daniel in the Bible. Because they were good-looking, showed intelligence in every branch of wisdom, and were endowed with understanding and discerning knowledge, they were included among the young men selected for service in the court of Babylon's King Nebuchadnezzar.

These four "golden chosen" were Daniel, Shadrach, Meshach, and Abednego. They had everything good at their disposal, and all they had to do was obey what the king said.

Then came a test from God.

Their culture and religious training had taught them the best diet to eat and drink. So when they were offered the king's richest diet of meat and wine, they refused it. But they were smart in how they declined. (Read the story in Daniel chapter 1.) They knew what would keep their bodies strong and their minds alert. And as a result of their sticking with God's diet plan and not yielding to the temptation of those fine meats and wine, they were rewarded by God with greater knowledge and intelligence in every branch of literature and wisdom; Daniel even understood all kinds of visions and used this gift to tell the king what his dreams meant.

Then came another test from God.

The king made an image of an idol and set it in the plains of Dura in the province of Babylon for all the people of his kingdom to worship. When the people heard the sound of music they were to fall down and worship the golden image. But Shadrach, Meshach, and Abednego, who worshiped the God of their fathers, refused to bow down. They recognized the lie of Satan and honored the living God, and Him only.

Some of the other guys, wanting favor from the king, squealed on these three, and the king got seriously mad. As punishment for anyone who did not bow down and worship the image, the king promised to throw them in a furnace so hot it would dissolve them to melted grease. ("Melted grease" is not actually a part of the story; that's just my take on the furnace. Read it for yourself in Daniel 3.)

These boys were bold enough to defy the king's order and stand together for their true God. They did not bow down to the idol, so they were thrown into that hot grease furnace to be French-fried to a crisp.

I know how it feels to be fried by hot grease. One summer day I spilled a deep fryer of hot fish grease, and some of the grease burned my arm with third-degree burns. I got so sick from those burns, I spent nine days in bed. Each time I look at the scars on my arm and remember how painful that was, I cringe to think of what could have happened to those three Hebrew boys had they not been rescued by Jesus Himself in that furnace. Those boys were saved by the God they worshiped because they were obedient to the laws and Word of God. Sure, they disobeyed the human king, but they obeyed the King of kings.

When the king of Babylon looked into the furnace for the three French-fried boys, he saw not three but *four* people inside there—and they were up and walking around like they were chilling on the beach. This freaked out the king and all his subjects who looked inside the furnace.

Those boys had stood up for right. Before they were thrown in the furnace, they made this declaration:

> If that is the case, our God whom we serve is able to deliver us from the burning fiery furnace, and He will deliver us from your hand, O king. But if not, let it be known to you, O king, that we do not serve your gods, nor will we worship the gold image which you have set up. (Daniel 3:17–18)

They stood up for what was right. God did not disappoint them. He saved them because of their obedience. When the king saw the power of God, he began to acknowledge the God of these Hebrew boys.

Attitudes of Obedience

Like those three, Daniel was also strong, bold, and committed to his God. Even though he had interpreted dreams for the king and was given high responsibilities in the kingdom, he too was tested.

After Belshazzar became king, he held a great feast for a thousand nobles. During the feast he praised the gods of gold and of silver, bronze, iron, wood, and stone. Suddenly a strange, unattached hand began to write on the wall, and this frightened the king and his partiers. The queen persuaded the king to call for Daniel to interpret the writing on the wall. Of course, Daniel was anointed for this job, and he told the king the truth. This created some furor, but the king had promised special gifts and privileges to Daniel if he explained what the writing meant (it was a message about God's judgment on the king), so Daniel was rewarded according to the king's promise. (Read about it in Daniel 5).

Daniel then served the next king, Darius, and served him well. Then came another time of testing.

Other commissioners and high officials in the kingdom convinced the king to issue an injunction that for thirty days anyone who made a petition to any god or man besides King Darius should be cast into a den of lions. Daniel, like his friends, worshiped Almighty God, the true God of their fathers, and he refused to stop worshiping and praying to Him.

The high officials reported this to King Darius. He was grieved, because he was forced by his own proclamation to put his loyal servant Daniel into the lions' den. It was a long sleepless night for the king.

But rejoicing came in the morning, when Darius and his party hurried to the lions' den to see anything that might be left of Daniel's remains. Lo and behold, Daniel was alive and well! (Can't you just see Daniel sitting there with his legs crossed, leaning back against a lion's mane, and singing "My

God Reigns"?) God had sent an angel and shut the lions' mouths. Daniel was saved.

At one point in the book of Daniel, we see a list of six attributes that characterized Daniel—all of them attitudes of obedience that we can adopt today. Here's what people observed in Daniel: "an excellent spirit, knowledge, understanding, interpreting dreams, solving riddles, and explaining enigmas [or "dissolving of doubts" (KJV)]" (Daniel 5:12).

God calls us to have "an excellent spirit" as well:

> And whatever you do, do it heartily, as to the Lord and not to men, knowing that from the Lord you will receive the reward of the inheritance; for you serve the Lord Christ. (Colossians 3:23–24)

As for "knowledge" and "understanding," the foundation for these is always the Word of God. Whatever we need to know, God has it in His Word. When we read and study the Bible, we must ask to be anointed with understanding so we can know what the Word is speaking in our hearts.

As for the other things in that description of Daniel, I'm reminded that God still gives some people the ability to interpret dreams; He still gifts others with the kind of discernment that lets them detect anything that may not be for our good; and when we trust in God with all our heart, it's easy to dissolve our doubts and fears and lean totally on Him.

Trying to Play God

When you're young like Bobby and the prodigal son, you think you're smarter than you are. The sin of arrogance is an illusive sin, and most of us deal with it. It makes you think you're so smart and cool. You feel like you have all the answers because you are intelligent and can read and write.

When I was young, my perspective was along these lines: "God gave us brains so we can think; we don't have to ask Him to do what *we* can do. So I should bother Him with only big things." And I'll bet (if I were a betting woman) that you've felt the same way, and maybe even heard some "genius" teach that very thing.

I didn't see a lot wrong with me until I started having conversations with God.

Often, when I made my decisions, they were not made with the best sense, but made out of emotion. Most of the time, I would make a mess of the situation. I couldn't understand why things were going the way they were. After all, I was a smart, intelligent college graduate. I knew what I was doing. It was all these other people I was dealing with who were creating the problem. (Listen to that lie of Satan: "Other people make me do the things I do"; "Other people make me say the things I say"; "I wish other people were as smart as I am, then they would understand what I'm trying to show them.")

So I've had to learn to totally lean on God.

Many of my personal and business relationships were rocky because I tried to handle everything on my own without consulting God, the Master Relationship Builder. I managed home and work, and thought I was great at both, only to discover that others viewed me as being demanding and controlling.

My husband would tell me I needed to stop trying to change him; he was not going to change for me, because he liked himself and he was the same man I married; so why did I want to change him?

He was right. (He didn't change, thank God; I really like him the way he is!) Flesh and blood did not reveal to me that he was right; *God* did, after years of me trying to play God and change my husband and the world.

I discovered I was not a great manager when one of the employees where I worked reported me to Human Relations. She told them, "Thelma never tells us when we do good, but if we make a mistake, she's all over us like a tent." When that report was presented to me, I was shocked. Me? What was she talking about? Could she be right? Oh my goodness, I thought I was the perfect manager.

These issues, among several, caused me to take a look at myself. I didn't see a lot wrong with me until I started having conversations with God. I asked Him to show me myself. In my mind I started documenting when I would correct someone or when I would struggle with something I didn't like or understand in my dealings with others (including my husband). I prayed more for guidance in what I did. I asked Him to change *me* if there was anything wrong. I asked Him to show me how to become the person He would be pleased with and the person who could help other people be better.

In other words, I learned that I didn't have all the sense—but God did.

So Many Sins—And So Much Forgiveness!

Have you learned to take a close look at yourself, as I did, and a close look at the sin that's really there?

(And remember that the sins of omission are just as bad as the sins of commission. If God has told us to do something and we don't, or if we know we should be doing something for the kingdom but we aren't, it is sin—just as much as the things we qualify as "big" sins. So, you're not exempt from the sin thing.)

I just hope you got wise early in your life and did not have to suffer so many consequences from sin. Myself...I could give you a list of my sins, but I've already given them to God through repentance, and He has forgiven me. No need to go over the list for you. However, you may want to think back, as I did, and search for those sins you have not confessed and repented of. It surely feels clean when you know you have been washed white as snow—that your sins have been washed away in the sea of forgetfulness (that last phrase is not in the Bible, but it sounds good). The truth is that "there is therefore now no condemnation to those who are in Christ Jesus, who do not walk according to the flesh, but according to the Spirit" (Romans 8:1).

I am so glad about that. Do you realize that because you are His child, none of the sins you've committed are condemned by Jesus? However, you are not off the hook as far as consequences go. God designed the universe with natural consequences for everything we do. If you do right, you have the natural consequences of being rewarded for right actions. If you do wrong (sin) you have the natural consequences of being punished.

It's the law of reciprocity. You reap what you sow.

Bobby and the prodigal son reaped the consequences of disobedience and rebellion. They made terrible choices that got them in trouble with the law, disrespected by family and friends, and humiliated and embarrassed in their spirit. Ultimately, when they saw the downward spiral of their lives, they humbled themselves and repented of their sins. As their good and gracious Father, God forgave them and caused their family members to forgive them. This state of forgiveness they attained can be enjoyed by all those who become wise and change their sinful ways. There is therefore no condemnation by Christ for these young men! (Shout hallelujah!)

In the time of Daniel, those young men could stand in a fiery furnace and come out without even the smell of smoke in their clothes. And although that kind of punishment doesn't exist in our society today, there's assurance in the Word of God that when we have accepted Christ Jesus as Lord and Savior, we can go through the fires of life and not be burned.

> "When you walk through the fire of oppression, you will not be burned up; the flames will not consume you. For I am the LORD, your God." (Isaiah 43:2–3, NLT)

Wow! Obedience really is better than anything else you could do.

Sin Is Sin

Okay, it's time to confess another sin of mine. I've been speaking, singing, and serving the Lord for most of my life and professionally for nearly thirty years. Wise people have been telling me to slow down, get some rest, learn to relax, stop taking on everybody's problems, take a real vacation, stop being a workaholic, eat right, and drink more water. Sure, that sounded good to me, and sometimes I would commit to doing just that.

However, I would find myself in the same whirlwind doing business as usual, in speed mode. Things had to get done, deadlines had to be met, relationships had to be bonded, people had to be counseled, and on and on. I emotionally refused to listen to the wise counsel I'd been given. This sin of ignoring God's prophets, and feeling so arrogantly necessary to the body of Christ, cost me months of sickness and disease. I battled cancer, lung problems, lower extremities trauma, fatigue, and severe arthritis—and during that time I missed some important speaking engagements and events.

What might have happened if I had listened to those who counseled me, rather than thinking myself invincible? More than likely, I would have experienced good health and the ability to do God's work with strength and stamina.

God knew just how much I needed to learn about doing His work His way. He took me through the process of serious illness and lengthy recovery for a purpose. He wanted me to obey Him in every situation. He wanted me to understand what it means to feel the awful pains of sickness as others feel, so I can authentically empathize with them. He wanted me to know that it is He who keeps me and orders my steps; I'm not in control of *anything.*

Sin is sin, whether you're a drug addict, prodigal, or rejecter of wise counsel. Anything that goes against God's law and His standards for our lives is SIN. He wants us to realize that, and He wants to teach us day by day to walk in righteousness.

Some of us with hard heads have to be taught this lesson: God is not through with us yet!

Your Journal

Write down your answer to this question: How can your own life change as you accept the truth that your obedience to the Lord is better than anything else you could do?

PART III

FOR YOUR REFLECTION

CHAPTER 12

THOUGHTS IN THE MORNING

I was just lying on my bed at 5:00 a.m. in the comfort and tranquility of my lake house, and thinking about what these past several months of health's ups and downs really mean to me.

I've never been afraid—not one minute. I've gotten disgusted with the fact that the old gray mare ain't what she used to be. I can't get up early in the morning and go 150 percent all day long like I once did. I've got to stop at about every three hours and rest. (Shucks!)

The time I've had to rest has become quiet time in the presence of the Lord, except on days when my grandchildren are around. Then it's escape-to-my-bedroom time to recuperate from playing, listening to stories, watching them develop their little relationships, and watching Barney until I'm almost purple. I can't knock those times though. They're some of the most precious times of my life. Just think, I get to teach them and leave a legacy at the same time. Now that I have ten grands and one great-grand, I can understand and appreciate the times my own great-grandmother spent with me.

Having been born to a crippled teenager in the early 1940s was not a beginning that promised success to this little black girl. Having a grandmother who did not want me in her sight (but also a granddaddy who loved both me and his fallen daughter) was a part of God's master plan for my success.

You see, we can't count anybody out of the game until the game is over. My granddaddy asked his aging mother if she would keep me and said he would help her all he could. This man of his word did just that. The two people I loved most in the world were my granddaddy and his mother, who raised me from two years old. This old lady set aside her declining years to instill in me the character, morals, dedication, and love of God that I can, in a greater way, pass on to my grandchildren.

So, knowing how God has guided every stage of my life, what have these past several months taught me?

God Is at Work for Our Good

I've learned and relearned that whatever happens in your life, good or not so good, God is working things out for our good, and He desires for us to see the good in everything. God never seeks our harm by putting heartache, sickness, disease, distress, fear, hurt, or any such thing upon us. Sure, He knows what we're going through, but He does not do us bad. He can't! God is a God of love, health, wellness, kindness, gentleness, and all good things.

Okay, there are places in the Bible where He often seems harsh. Yes, in the Old Testament He brought famine and exile and many devastating things upon His people—but it was because He simply wanted them to love and trust Him. He was trying to show them His power.

It has been said that the Old Testament is Jesus concealed, while the New Testament is Jesus revealed. And what Jesus has revealed is a fuller picture of God and His love and His power. Jesus now comes into the hearts of every believer through the power of His death, burial, resurrection, and ascension. On the cross, God gave Jesus the ability and authority to take up our sins and afflictions and griefs and despair, and to bear all these so we would not have to do it for ourselves. God knew we didn't have it in us! Jesus paid it all, and all to Him we owe!

The blood of Jesus that was shed for our redemption from sin covers all the hurtful issues of our mortal lives, including our afflictions. Don't forget what He said to Paul regarding his thorn in the flesh: "My grace is sufficient for you." And in everything we encounter, throughout life's ups and downs, He is saying to us, "Sweetie, don't you know that My grace is sufficient for your circumstances?"

He Keeps Us Alive to Do His Work

I've also learned that all sickness is not unto death, regardless of how it may look to the natural eye.

My doctor told me that he thought I was a goner during the second surgery. My lungs collapsed, I had tremendous trauma to my body because of the exposure of my intestines, and I was on life support (none of which I remember, because I was asleep all that time). But when God is not through with you yet, I don't care what the doctors say or how it looks, God will bring you through. I'm here today because there were and are things God wants me to understand, know, and do that could not be accomplished with me dead. He had communicated to me some of those things, and what God says is perfect and true.

So think of the dangers, toils, and snares He's brought *you* through. Why did He do it? Because He ain't through with you either.

Some Will Not Understand Your Conversations with God

I've learned that when the Lord is dealing with you, you don't need a lot of people around you who don't believe like you believe. You see, you really can't tell a lot of people about the conversations between you and the Lord, because they think you're either super-religious or borderline crazy.

When I would try to begin telling some people what the Lord was saying to me and how He was dealing with me, they would look at me patronizingly and give me a faint smile as if to say, "Poor lady, she's lost it." Not so. I *found* it! I found that God would really speak to me with His still, small voice like my great-grandmother used to speak to me. (Yeah, I probably looked at her the same way people looked at me; she just didn't know it, because I would have faced negative consequences if I looked at her like I thought she was lying.)

As I've faced this issue in recent months, it bothered me at first because I could not understand how *they* could not understand what I was trying to say. Then it happened: I woke up to the revelation that God was talking to *me,* not them. He tells them what He wants to, and me what He wants to, and what He tells me is not always to be told. Hello...I woke up! It got a lot easier then to keep things to myself.

My husband has said, "If you don't want it in a book, don't tell my wife." Now, is that nice? No, but it's pretty accurate. Now I've almost learned to keep me and God's conversations private, because He tells me in private. There are, however, some things I can reveal, like messages that He gives me to tell the people. Boy, He has filled my head and heart with truth from His Word, and I'm still basking in and studying His Word because some messages have to go out that can revolutionize the minds of many. Oh me, I started to tell you one—but remembered it's not developed yet, so I need to keep quiet until the time He has given me to tell it.

People Can't Care for You Like God Can

I've learned too that when you first get sick, people are interested in knowing how you're doing and they send cards, come visit you, pray for you, and are concerned about you. But when you stay sick a long time, people have their own lives to live, and their attentiveness wanes. Therefore, you should never depend on other people to keep your spirits up. That's not their job; it's *God's* job, and He does it really well. I know, because He has kept my spirits up for all these months, and He keeps on improving them.

I heard someone say that *you* are the only person responsible for your emotions. So true!

So get over looking for everyone else to help you feel good. It ain't their job, baby. They can't even keep themselves feeling good all the time, without the help of the Lord. So get over yourself and what you expect from other people. They have their own life to live just like you do.

> *You should never depend on other people to keep your spirits up. That's God's job, and He does it really well.*

Do you remember all those times you were interested in helping someone in need for a limited time, then you went on to the next person? Life does not revolve around any one of us; therefore, lift up your eyes to the hills from whence comes your help; your help comes from the Lord who made heaven and earth (see Psalm 121).

We Must Abide

And I've learned that we cannot pray appropriately unless we abide in Him.

Abiding in God means to eat the Word of God so that every situation is saturated in the Word. And when we abide and pray the Word, God answers our prayers according to His perfect will for our lives.

He wishes above all things that we would spiritually prosper and be in health. He knows the plans He has for our lives, that they are plans for our well-being and not for calamity; His plans are for a rich future and a bright hope for us (see Jeremiah 29:11).

For every situation I encountered during these months of affliction and recovery, there has been a word concerning it in the Bible. When I studied that word—not just read it, but spent some time studying it—I found that the applications of the word were ways I should pray. Praying in the abiding Word of God brought victory, even though it did not look like it sometimes, and even though the first verdict was not what I expected God to do. He had a better plan to show all involved that He is in charge.

We must remember that when we pray, if other people are involved, God knows what they need and where they are in the situation, and He works out all things (and people) according to His will.

Studying the Word of God gives great power to our being because in His Word we get the recipe for godly living. So it's imperative that we are studying the Word daily. "Oh, taste and see that the LORD is good" (Psalm 34:8). Missing the daily study of the Word is like missing breakfast, lunch, and dinner. When you miss all those meals for a day—unless you're on a spiritual fast and the Lord keeps you—you will be so weak that you can't think or talk. Well, sugar, I don't miss many meals. The one thing I can always do, whatever is happening around me, is eat. The importance of my meals now is second to the importance of my study of the Word.

The Word of God strengthens you for the tasks ahead. The Word of God has anointing power to help you meet life's challenges. The Word of God speaks to your spirit and interprets some of the mysteries of God to you. The Word of God illuminates the power of the risen Savior to you and tells you your worth in Him. The Word of God shows up your weaknesses and shortcomings and allows you the right as a child of God to repent and regain your rightful place in heavenly places with Jesus. The Word of God teaches about morals, values, character, and right living to the point that there is no shadow of turning into the sinful creature we can all be. The Word of God helps you not be flaky about your faith by running after every new fad or trend that comes into the religious circles of today. The Word of God tells you where we are in Bible history and what to look for as the world turns. The Word of God teaches you how to run your businesses and how to be a great employee. The Word of God explains how you are to be a steward over what He has allowed you to have and how you are to be a blessing to others. The Word of God teaches how to manage your money, time, energy, and relationships. The Word of God shows how to respond to authorities that are over you. The Word of God offers everything you need to know to help you live free from stress and distress in this life.

Now don't you want to spend more time in it? I do. There is no way in this lifetime I can understand everything in His Word, but I can sure try the best I can to understand everything I can while I can.

What a Savior!

The biggest thing I've learned is that an intimate relationship with God through Jesus His Son is the best thing that has ever happened to me. There is absolutely nothing that Jesus and I cannot talk about. He works it all out; I just tell Him. After I tell Him, I praise and worship Him, because I realize that He is moved by my praise of Him. Before and after every successful battle in the Bible that I have experienced in my time with Him in these recent months, there was praise and worship going on.

Oh, how I love Jesus! Oh, can't nobody do me like Jesus! Oh, what a Savior He is! Glorify His holy name. Magnify His holy name. Praise His holy name. Respect His holy name. Honor His holy name.

I surrender to His holy name. I will always respect and adore His holy name...because God is not through with me yet!

SPECIAL SECTION I

CHRIST THE I AM

Jesus made some great claims—not just about His abilities, as many often do, but about His own character and nature.

Some have characterized these claims as posing a dilemma for mankind: Is He Lord, liar, or lunatic? Of course, only one of these choices is defensible.

When Jesus came into the world, the world was essentially ignorant of God—just as we are without knowing Jesus. But in all that Jesus did, He was showing us God (John 14:8–10).

So let's learn more deeply who Jesus is—and become more convinced that He is the eternal Lord—by walking through some Scriptures and looking closely at His own words.

THE ETERNAL ONE

When we think rightly of I AM, Jesus is always included. We can easily see why in John's Gospel.

In John 8, after the Jews accused Jesus of being demonic (vv. 48–52), Jesus actually claims the name of God given to Moses in the burning bush. I hope familiarity with Scripture has not blunted our ability to be amazed by this claim:

> Jesus said to them, "Most assuredly, I say to you, before Abraham was, I AM." (John 8:58)

His listeners on that occasion knew full well what the Scriptures revealed about this name:

> God said to Moses, "I AM WHO I AM." And He said, "Thus you shall say to the children of Israel, 'I AM has sent me to you.'" (Exodus 3:14)

Because Jesus was making such a bold claim—claiming as His own name the revealed name of the Lord God—the Jews were outraged enough that they "took up stones to throw at Him" (John 8:59). They were refusing to accept what all who are truly saved have come to believe: Jesus is eternal God, just as John's Gospel tells us at the very beginning.

In the beginning was the Word, and the Word was with God, and the Word was God. He was in the beginning with God. All things were made through Him, and without Him nothing was made that was made. In Him was life, and the life was the light of men. . . .

And the Word became flesh and dwelt among us, and we beheld His glory, the glory as of the only begotten of the Father, full of grace and truth. (John 1:1–4, 14)

John's Gospel Shows the Way

Besides those amazing words in John 8, we see Jesus making seven other key "I AM" statements throughout John's Gospel, in which He reveals Himself to be the Son of God who brings eternal life.

Consequently, we can know Jesus as:
I AM the Bread of Life (John 6:35, 48)
I AM the Light of the World (John 8:12; 9:5)
I AM the Door (John 10:7, 9)
I AM the Good Shepherd (John 10:11, 14)
I AM the Resurrection and the Life (John 11:25)
I AM the Way, the Truth, and the Life (John 14:6)
I AM the True Vine (John 15:1, 5)

These seven I AM declarations signify a new beginning for mankind. They emphasize the purpose of the Book of John, and they reveal the true relationship of Jesus to mankind and of mankind to Jesus.

That's why, when I speak of I AM's authority to create my ability to work for Him, Jesus is always included.

He Is the Bread of Life

> I am the bread of life. He who comes to Me shall never hunger, and he who believes in Me shall never thirst. . . .
>
> I am the bread of life. (John 6:35, 48)

When Jesus spoke these words, He was trying to warn people against the limited view that is concerned only with the material.

Jesus is the sustainer of Life:

> The thief does not come except to steal, and to kill, and to destroy. I have come that they may have life, and that they may have it more abundantly. (John 10:10)

Jesus is not only the Bread of Life; He tells us He is also the Water of Life:

> If anyone thirsts, let him come to Me and drink. He who believes in Me, as the Scripture has said, out of his heart will flow rivers of living water. (John 7:37–38)

If we drink this Water of Life, we will never thirst again, just as Jesus assured the woman at the well:

> If you knew the gift of God, and who it is who says to you, "Give Me a drink," you would have asked Him, and He would have given you living water. (John 4:10)

With Jesus, life is satisfying; without Him, it is meaningless.

So many people feed on husks...when the Lord has provided a feast with only good things—good *for* you too.

Why did the prodigal leave home? He wanted *life*—but he interpreted life in terms of the material. Yet he finally came to see a greater need of his life. Tragically, some never see this greater need—they only vaguely feel the discontent.

He Is the Light of the World

> I am the light of the world. He who follows Me shall not walk in darkness, but have the light of life. (John 8:12)

> As long as I am in the world, I am the light of the world. (John 9:5)

Jesus came into a world of darkness—to people plunged into darkness by sin.

He came into this darkness as the Light, just as the Scriptures prophesied:

> For behold, the darkness shall cover the earth, and deep darkness the people; but the LORD will arise over you, and His glory will be seen upon you. (Isaiah 60:2)

God promised them glorious times when they would no longer be in the gloomy darkness:

> The LORD will be your everlasting light, and the days of your mourning shall be ended. (Isaiah 60:20)

This moment became a reality with Jesus:

> In Him was life, and the life was the light of men. And the light shines in the darkness, and the darkness did not comprehend it. (John 1:4–5)

Just as the Hebrews, as they traveled out of Egypt, were led by the pillar of fire by night and the cloud by day, so Jesus, today, leads all who will see, so that we can express our gratitude with these words:

> Your word is a lamp to my feet and a light to my path.... The entrance of Your words gives light; it gives understanding to the simple. (Psalm 119:105, 130)

When Jesus opened a blind man's eyes, He was enacting a living parable of His real mission, just as His words on this occasion confirmed: "As long as I am in the world, I am the light of the world" (John 9:5).

And yet—so many people stumble in the darkness, when the light switch is at hand!

He Is the Door

> Most assuredly, I say to you, I am the door of the sheep. . . .
>
> I am the door. If anyone enters by Me, he will be saved, and will go in and out and find pasture. (John 10:7, 9)

Jesus lets his sheep in and keeps predators out. He welcomes us and He protects us from intruders.

He Is the Good Shepherd

And so, Jesus is the Good Shepherd.

> I am the good shepherd. The good shepherd gives His life for the sheep. . . .
>
> I am the good shepherd; and I know My sheep, and am known by My own. (John 10:11, 14)

Human beings have always needed such a shepherd to show them the way, just as the prophet Jeremiah affirmed:

> O Lord, I know the way of man is not in himself; it is not in man who walks to direct his own steps. (Jeremiah 10:23)

The history of Israel and the whole world provides evidence of this.

So Jesus comes to provide guidance. His care and concern is as the owner, not as a hireling.

And He knows us *individually.* "My sheep hear My voice, and I know them, and they follow Me" (John 10:27).

This Shepherd is *good,* and He shows His goodness in His willingness to die for the sheep. Others (like the Pharisees and Sadducees) would sell the sheep for their own benefit. But Jesus, the Good Shepherd, "gives His life for the sheep" (John 10:11).

In this passage Jesus also says, "Therefore My Father loves Me, because I lay down My life that I may take it again" (John 10:17). For the sake of the helpless sheep, Jesus lays down His life (showing His goodness), so that He could later take it up again (in His resurrection, showing His divinity).

He Is the Resurrection and Life

> I am the resurrection and the life. He who believes in Me, though he may die, he shall live. (John 11:25)

The great pyramids of Egypt are monuments to man's efforts to provide for the next life. Not so impressive, but just as illustrative, are the flowers and artifacts found in the graves of primitive man. All of this is mute witness to man's desire for and belief in a life hereafter.

But not until Jesus came did we have confidence in the reality of such an everlasting life, or know why we should even hope for one. Even the wisest man, Solomon, did not know for certain—he only dimly thought of the possibility of life after death as evidenced by his writings in Ecclesiastes.

Jesus, however, clearly promises us eternal life:

> This is the will of the Father who sent Me, that of all He has given Me I should lose nothing, but should *raise it up at the last day.* (John 6:39)

> And this is the will of Him who sent Me, that everyone who sees the Son and believes in Him may have everlasting life; and *I will raise him up at the last day*....
>
> No one can come to Me unless the Father who sent Me draws him; and *I will raise him up at the last day*....
>
> Whoever eats My flesh and drinks My blood has eternal life, and *I will raise him up at the last day.* (John 6:40, 44, 54)

And His own resurrection is proof of His capacity to make and keep this promise.

> Jesus answered and said to them, "Destroy this temple, and in three days I will raise it up." Then the Jews said, "It has taken forty-six years to build this temple, and will You raise it up in three days?" But He was speaking of the temple of His body. (John 2:19–21)

> Therefore My Father loves Me, because I lay down My life that I may take it again. (John 10:17)

Resurrection and life can be *ours* in Him, because Jesus Himself *is* resurrection and life. Resurrection is but an incident; the greater reality is that He is life. Jesus both created life (John 1:1–3) and sustains life—for He is the One "upholding all things by the word of His power" (Hebrews 1:3).

He Is the Way, the Truth, and the Life

> I am the way, the truth, and the life. No one comes to the Father except through Me. (John 14:6)

This wonderful statement was given in answer to a question from the disciple Thomas:

> Thomas said to Him, "Lord, we do not know where You are going, and how can we know the way?" (John 14:5)

This is the Thomas who will not pretend all is well when it is not, nor pretend he believes when he does not, nor pretend he knows when he does not. And to this Thomas, Jesus reveals this dynamic reality about Himself.

Not only does Jesus reveal the Father, but He provides us a way to Him, as the prophetic Scriptures foretold:

> A highway shall be there, and a road, and it shall be called the Highway of Holiness.... But the redeemed shall walk there, and the ransomed of the LORD shall return. (Isaiah 35:8–10)

Jesus is the way *because* He is the truth, and truth makes one free:

> And you shall know the truth, and the truth shall make you free.... Therefore if the Son makes you free, you shall be free indeed. (John 8:32, 36)

In God is no lie; Jesus is the way *because* He is life:

> For as the Father raises the dead and gives life to them, even so the Son gives life to whom He will....For as the Father has life in Himself, so He has granted the Son to have life in Himself. (John 5:21, 26)

As the true Life, Jesus "is before all things, and in Him all things consist" (Colossians 1:17).

Jesus showed us how to live in unity with the Father. Jesus, indeed, is the only legitimate way to God, despite other claims by misguided men.

Yes, there is a way...but so many will not walk it.

He Is the Vine

> I am the true vine, and My Father is the vinedresser....

> I am the vine, you are the branches. He who abides in Me, and I in him, bears much fruit; for without Me you can do nothing. (John 15:1, 5)

Jesus had a great work for His disciples (and us) to do. How could they (and we) accomplish it?

Only because He Himself nurtures His followers in this task.

We cannot bear fruit apart from Him. We bear fruit only because we are *in Him.* This kind of relationship demands that we *abide* in Him.

God looks for fruit from His efforts among His people (see the prophetic parable in Isaiah 5:1–7). But *He Himself* produces the fruit through us, not expecting us to bring about on our own that which we are not capable of.

Jesus calls Himself "the true vine," while He tells us that His Father is "the vinedresser" (or "the gardener" or "the husbandmen," as other versions put it). This work is too important to entrust to anyone else.

Prayer is a continuous part of this abiding and fruit-bearing process, as Jesus goes on to say:

> If you abide in Me, and My words abide in you, you will ask what you desire, and it shall be done for you. (John 15:7)

To "ask" here is to "demand as your due"; that's the meaning of the word in the original language. This is one of the strongest promises in Scripture concerning prayer. The central focus is fruit bearing, and it does not concern prayer which doesn't focus on fruit bearing.

The result of all this is that we get to experience His joy:

> These things I have spoken to you, that My joy may remain in you, and that your joy may be full. (John 15:11)

This is the very first time in the book of John that Jesus speaks of His joy—and He does it in this moment when His torture will be beginning in only a few hours!

He is the true vine, the unfailing vine. Have you put your trust in Him? Are you abiding in Him? If you will, you will then bear fruit.

Conclusion

So what do you think of Jesus?

Is He Lord, liar, or lunatic? If either of the latter two, then dismiss Him and all that He said—if you can.

If not—if He is indeed Lord—then surrender to Him now.

Your Journal

Write down your answer to this question: How can your own life change as you realize more and more that your Lord and Savior Jesus is the I AM, the eternal God?

SPECIAL SECTION 2

SECRETS OF PRAYER

Prayer is expressing yourself to God in whatever way you know how. That's why I said earlier in this book that if you can talk, you can pray.

There are, however, some effective tools to learn about and use when praying.

PRAY GOD'S WORD

The most important tool is Scripture. Learn to pray the Word of God.

When we pray, praying the Word of God is effective and on-target and always appropriate. When you pray the Scriptures in the correct context, you're always praying God's will.

Sometimes, when people ask me to pray for them and I don't know the circumstances or the parties involved in their request, I'll simply pray the Word.

For example:

"Father, in the name of Jesus, I pray according to Proverbs 3:5–6 that (insert the name) will trust in You with all their heart and lean not on their own understanding. I pray that in all their ways, they will acknowledge You, and I know You will direct their paths."

I will also pray according to the events and stories that are there in Scripture as an example for us:

"Master Healer, I ask in Jesus' name that You will heal the cancer in (insert the name). Your Word reveals that You can heal every disease, for healing virtue can flow from Your body as it did when You healed the woman with the issue of blood in Matthew 9:21. I stand on Your Word."

I will also pray the Word for myself:

"O Lord, my Provider, Your Word says that if I give according to Your Word, You will give back to me good measure, pressed down, shaken together, and running over. I trust this promise of Yours in Luke 6:38, and I expect the blessings, in Jesus' name."

There is power in praying the Word of God because His Word is the only thing that will last throughout this world and the world to come.

God is still teaching me how to pray—because God is not through with me yet! As I mentioned earlier, on one unforgettable occasion God spoke to me in my mind and told me, "I am going to teach you to really pray for one year; then I will release you to pray for kings and queens of the nations." To help me intercede in this way, He's teaching me daily to pray the Scriptures over every situation, and then to watch Him keep His Word.

Pray in Spirit and Truth

Another thing to learn about prayer is to pray in the Holy Spirit (see Ephesians 6:18 and Jude 20). Jesus told us to pray without doubting and with confidence, believing that God will hear and answer our prayers. The Holy Spirit gives us that confidence and guides us in what we are to pray—and He should never be ignored. Trust the Spirit to help you pray the perfect will of the Father.

We are to pray in the same way Jesus says we're to worship: "in spirit and truth" (John 4:24). When we pray *in truth,* we come before the Master honestly and without pretense. Even if we're disappointed with God and we wonder why our lives are not going the way we want, our attitude needs to be authentic as we come before Him.

Prayer is to be an expression of the heart's sincere desire. The optimum word there is *sincere,* and that sincerity must be accompanied with a condition of truth that the motives and actions of the prayer are in accordance with God's standards.

It is a fact that God is sovereign and can hear and answer anyone. It's really God's business whom He answers and whom He doesn't. But the overwhelming context for answered prayer is summed up in the condition of our heart. When the heart is not in tune with the heart of God, there can be many various hindrances and delays in our prayers.

Hindrances to Prayer

There are several factors that can hinder our prayers. *Sin* is at the top of my list of these.

What is sin? Sin is anything that is contrary to God's order. For example, we are told in the Bible not to lie, steal, cheat, covet, take the name of the Lord in vain, murder, worship idols, or desire unnatural affections. We are taught in Scripture to not be prideful, arrogant, boastful, angry, troublemakers, lustful, lazy, judgmental, greedy, hypocritical, out of fellowship with our spouse and others, or unforgiving. I could go on and on.

When the condition of our heart is bound by such sins, we hinder the answering of our prayers. In other words, unconfessed sin can stop God's answers, as He Himself has explained:

> Behold, the LORD's hand is not shortened, that it cannot save; nor His ear heavy, that it cannot hear.

> But your iniquities have separated you from your God; and your sins have hidden His face from you, so that He will not hear. (Isaiah 59:1–2)

The fact that God will not hear the requests that are prayed through a sinful heart is found also in Psalm 66:18: "If I regard iniquity in my heart, the Lord will not hear."

When we pray, we must ask God to forgive us. There's not one of us who doesn't have to ask God's forgiveness for sinning. Our sin might be an evil thought or something we said that we should not have. It could be something we failed to do when the Holy Spirit was directing us to do it. Whatever it might be, asking God's forgiveness can get us back into right standing with God to get our prayers answered.

In the Lord's Prayer, the phrase "Forgive us our debts as we forgive our debtors" is significant. It indicates that forgiveness is one of the right heart conditions for answered prayer—that we must be willing to forgive those who have wronged us. If we are not willing to forgive others, God has no obligation to forgive us or to answer our prayers.

Jesus says, "If you forgive men their trespasses, your heavenly Father will also forgive you. But if you do not forgive men their trespasses, neither will your Father forgive your trespasses" (Matthew 6:14–15). Therefore pray to God in the name of Jesus and confess your sins. He is faithful and just to forgive those sins and to attend to your needs.

Another hindrance to prayer is *wrong motives*. I've been in conversation with people who have commented (jokingly or not) that they have prayed for God to hurt somebody because they did not like them.

Come on, do you actually think God operates like that? Absolutely not!

The mother of James and John asked Jesus to grant her sons special privilege in the kingdom of God. Her request was for her sons to be better than anyone else. This kind of pride, arrogance, and haughtiness can hinder God's answers to prayer.

So can an overbearing attitude toward others, or thinking of yourself as better than others (selfishness). As James declares, "You ask and do not receive, because you ask amiss, that you may spend it on your pleasures" (James 4:3).

To get our prayers answered, we must be sure that the motives for our prayers are righteous and pure. The only way to have pure motives is to have the mind of Christ. This is possible if you know Him as your personal Lord and Savior and begin to think as He thinks. (If you keep the phrase "What would Jesus do?" in your thoughts, it can help you focus on Christ and not on your own selfish motives and desires.)

Therefore "put on the Lord Jesus Christ, and make no provision for the flesh, to fulfill its lusts" (Romans 13:14).

Unbelief is another hindrance to prayer. So often we're so childish in the way we refuse to believe what God tells us to avoid.

I'm intrigued by little children's curiosity about electrical plugs. As toddlers, they'll see the outlets in the wall and proceed to explore them. When they're told not to play with them, their curiosity only increases, and they head for them again.

In the same way, we "explore" dangers we've been warned about and ignore the fact that our Guardian who gave us the warnings is watching out for our well-being.

Often we do not believe God answers our prayers because we cannot see the immediate shock waves caused by our prayers. We cannot understand why our prayers are not answered the second we prayed. If the answer does not come quickly, we whine and develop an attitude of unbelief. When this happens, we may go through the motion of praying, but our prayers are from a double-minded, unstable, and wavering mindset.

Without believing, you cannot expect to receive. There is no faith when you don't believe. Trust God and know that whenever you pray, God is working behind the scenes to work it out for you.

Maybe you have been praying for something for years. Never give up! Always believe that the God who knows all and is in all has your heart at stake. He will not leave you or forsake you. When you can't see what He's doing, trust His heart that He will work it out.

GETTING GOD'S ANSWERS

Maybe you're still troubled by this thought: "I asked God for something, and He has not answered me yet." It's hard for you to accept that God answers our prayers in His own time, and His time is not our time.

Remember that God answers prayers in several ways. Sometimes He says *yes*. Sometimes He says *no*. Sometimes He says *wait*.

Talking to God is like talking to a good parent. If a child asks for something that will do the child good in that moment, the good parent will say yes. If a child asks for something harmful to that child, the good parent will say no. If the child asks for something the child is not ready for, even though it may be good for them, the answer may be wait. God answers the same way, because He is the best Father anyone can have.

Before there was ever a star in the sky, God already had our circumstances worked out and our prayers answered. There is no particular timing with God, because He is the

Alpha and the Omega, the Beginning and the End to all things in the universe. Nothing surprises God—not the good, the bad, or the ugly. He knows our innermost thoughts, all our actions and reactions. He is the Almighty God who sees, knows, listens, hears, and responds to our every word.

The fact that we cannot see God's answers is not an indication that He is not in the process of revealing His answer to us. He's always working behind the scenes to work things out for the good of those who love Him and are called according to His purposes.

Maybe I'm praying for a person's healing, and that person has decided they want the ultimate healing—death. Perhaps I'm praying for a loved one to be saved and they refuse to accept Jesus as their Savior. There might be a broken relationship that I want mended but the other person is rejecting my desires.

God understands all the people and circumstances in our prayers, and He works things out according to what is good for all of us when we submit ourselves to His perfect will.

Recently, I had two vibrant friends die from cancer. Many of us prayed and prayed and prayed for their healing. Both of these ladies gave up their will to live and consequently died early deaths for their ages. Why would God not answer our prayer? He certainly could have; He has the power to do anything (except fail). He could have even changed their will to die to a will to live. But He didn't.

God has said that the days of our lives are numbered, and only He knows when our time on this earth is over. It would be futile for me to get angry with God for not answering our prayers the way we wanted Him to, because He knows the end from the beginning. He allowed my two friends the privilege of understanding that their time was about over, and they both died in dignity, leaving a legacy of a life well lived. God was ready for them, and they were ready for God.

We can't understand God's timing; we *can* know that He never makes a mistake. God does not answer all prayers the way I want Him to. But even when He doesn't, I've always experienced a great lesson or something better as results.

Acknowledging God

God is a God of order. He does not do anything just for the sake of doing it. He has a master plan for our prayer life that includes our attitudes and our reasons for praying.

That master plan for prayer includes the fact that *we must acknowledge God, our Father in heaven*. Our acknowledgement of God honors and respects God's good name, His character, His integrity, His sovereignty, and His power as our heavenly Father.

Don't forget the beginning of the prayer Jesus taught His disciples ("The Lord's Prayer"): "Our Father in heaven, hallowed be Your name" (Matthew 6:9). Acknowledging God as holy opens the door for Him to communicate with His children.

What father does not want to be honored and respected? When we honor our earthly fathers, a bond of unity is established that creates a closeness one can hardly express. Our attitude toward God should be established at the onset to clear the way for our open communication with the Father of the universe.

Rely on Christ's Intercession

We must also support our prayers by the intercession of Jesus, the Son of God, who holds the position of heavenly intercessor to the Father on our behalf. He is seated at the right hand of the throne of God praying for us to His Father.

When I pray, I like to think that Jesus says something like this to God: "Father, Thelma is in need of peace in her spirit. You promised that You would give her perfect peace if she keeps her mind on Me. Her mind is set on Me because I see her studying Your Word, applying Your principles, learning Your precepts, and recognizing Your Lordship. Please, Sir, give her instant peace." I believe right then and there the peace of God comes over me, and I calm down and begin to think clearly.

Jesus is our High Priest and has direct access to Deity. He is like the people He represents (you and me) because He came to earth as a man and lived among men, experiencing everything and anything we experience. He understands our hurt, pain, sorrows, joy, excitement, and happiness. There's nothing we go through that He cannot relate to. He is different from us because He is Righteousness and Truth. So when we approach God's throne through Jesus, we're there to receive mercy, grace, and help in our time of need.

Often people go to an earthly priest to confess their sins or discuss their issues. But priests cannot fully relate or understand, because of their own limitations. Jesus has no limitations. As our great High Priest, Jesus listens and attends to our confessions. In fact, Jesus is the only priest, pastor, minister, prophet, or bishop who can do us everlasting good. When we pray, therefore, we need to pray in the name of Jesus. We can be assured that when we do, Jesus attends to us and prays for us. We never pray alone. We pray with our great High Priest:

> Seeing then that we have a great High Priest who has passed through the heavens, Jesus the Son of

> God, let us hold fast our confession. For we do not have a High Priest who cannot sympathize with our weaknesses, but was in all points tempted as we are, yet without sin. Let us therefore come boldly to the throne of grace, that we may obtain mercy and find grace to help in time of need. (Hebrews 4:14–16)

That just sums it up. When you've got Jesus praying for you, you don't need anybody else. Hallelujah!

RELY ON THE SPIRIT'S INTERCESSION

I am blown away by the orderliness of God. Not only has He provided for us a heavenly intercessor in Jesus, He has also provided for us an earthly intercessor, the Holy Spirit.

In Romans 8:26–27 God anticipated that we would plead weakness or ignorance or give some excuse about how we can't pray and don't know how to pray. So the all-knowing God provided for us an earthly Advocate to live inside us to guide us in our prayers.

Listen to this:

> Likewise the Spirit also helps in our weaknesses. For we do not know what we should pray for as we ought, but the Spirit Himself makes intercession

> for us with groanings which cannot be uttered. Now He who searches the hearts knows what the mind of the Spirit is, because He makes intercession for the saints according to the will of God.

The Holy Spirit always interprets our prayers to the Father in accordance with the will of God. The Holy Spirit helps us understand God's will for our lives.

When we accept Jesus as our personal Lord and Savior, the Holy Spirit comes to live in our hearts. This Holy Spirit of God is the person who convicts us when we do wrong, comforts us when we are sad, and guides us in what we do. We are so fortunate that God loves us enough to never leave us powerless, to never leave us without help.

This same Holy Spirit who indwells us is our advocate in heaven. Wow!

So we have two great, high, and holy Advocates—Jesus and the Holy Spirit—always working in unison to bring us into the presence and glory of God our Father.

If you have been feeling alone and unable to pray, trust the fact that you have Jesus and the Holy Spirit overshadowing any insecurity you may have about praying to God. On your side you have two Friends in the most potent, powerful positions in the universe, making your situation known to and resolved by the Father.

Your Journal

Write down your answer to this question: How can your own life truly change as you pray in the way your Lord instructs you to pray?

Special Section 3

HEALING SCRIPTURES

There are dozens of healing accounts detailed in the Gospels and in Acts. Beyond that, there are a great many other Bible verses that relate in one way or another to this important topic.

So when I get e-mails, letters, or phone calls from those who are ill, or speak with them face-to-face, I offer them the healing Scriptures listed below, plus comments such as those you see along with the verses.

Before you get into these encouraging Scriptures, please remember that we have to balance the fact that God wants us healed with the fact that some Christians are not healed in their natural bodies, and not everybody lives to be seventy or eighty.

So why does God *not* heal every believer who lives according to the Scriptures?

I don't have the answers to this. I *do* know that God is sovereign and in control of everything. Yet sometimes little babies, and children, and young people will die from sickness and disease just as old people do.

I believe this is included in the mysteries that the Scriptures indicate are a part of our experience here: "The secret things belong to the LORD our God" (Deuteronomy 29:29); "For now we see in a mirror, dimly" (1 Corinthians 13:12); "It is not for you to know" (Acts 1:7); "You will understand hereafter" (John 13:7, NASB).

One thing I know for sure is that we should never blame God for not being healed on this earth. The apostle Paul had a thorn in his side (we don't know what it was, but some believe it was sickness). God did not deliver him, but Paul's most profound experience was the certainty that *God's grace is sufficient* for our every affliction.

Recently I sent an e-mail to my accountability partner, Debra Young. I assured her I was well and whole in my spirit, and I was physically on the mend, but my total healing had not been manifested. "There is never a day that I am not in some kind of pain," I told her. "I know God can heal me right this instant.... I also know that He walks with me every day through these trials."

Debra responded by saying, "This I know, that healing always comes.... Therefore we walk into it; sometimes more speedily than at other times." She cited promises of healing in Scripture and mentioned how "during prayer in the Spirit, I asked for wisdom on how to accelerate the supernatural, finished work. The answer as I understood it: 'Apply, apply…appropriate, appropriate.'" Debra was reminding me that application and appropriation of God's Word is what it takes to "faith it out" — getting our heart to totally agree with the Word of God so we experience life-impacting power in our journey through affliction.

The information below explains the Word of God that is true, firm, and strong, and will live forever. I believe in God, and though I am not fully healed physically from all of my sicknesses and afflictions, *I know God can do it.* Even if He doesn't, and instead of being physically restored I get the ultimate healing (death), I'm a winner either way. I get the best of this world with exceeding joy if I remain alive; I get the greatest reward ever in heaven if I die. Neither of these results negates the fact that *God wants us well*!

Promises of Health, Healing, and Life

- And the Lord will take away from you all sickness, and will afflict you with none of the terrible diseases of Egypt which you have known, but will lay them on all those who hate you. (Deuteronomy 7:15)

Note: This was a promise to God's covenant people under the Old Covenant—so how much more does this benefit of health pertain to us today who are under the New Covenant, which is based upon the precious blood of Jesus Christ!

- Many are the afflictions of the righteous, but the LORD delivers him out of them all. (Psalm 34:19)
- Why are you cast down, O my soul? And why are you disquieted within me? Hope in God; for I shall yet praise Him, the help of my countenance and my God. (Psalm 42:11)
- Bless the LORD, O my soul, and forget not all His benefits: who forgives all your iniquities, who heals all your diseases. (Psalm 103:2–3)

  Note: Notice it doesn't say "some"; it says "all"! This passage also states that healing is one of the benefits that belongs to the believer along with having our sins forgiven.
- But those who wait on the LORD shall renew their strength; they shall mount up with wings like eagles, they shall run and

not be weary, they shall walk and not faint. (Isaiah 40:31)

Note: The word *wait* in this verse implies a positive action of hope, based on knowing that the Word of God is a true fact and that it will soon come to pass. This is waiting with earnest expectation!

- Fear not, for I am with you; be not dismayed, for I am your God. I will strengthen you, yes, I will help you, I will uphold you with My righteous right hand. (Isaiah 41:10)
- Surely He has borne our griefs [literally "sicknesses"] and carried our sorrows; yet we esteemed Him stricken, smitten by God, and afflicted. But He was wounded for our transgressions, He was bruised for our iniquities; the chastisement for our peace was upon Him, and by His stripes we are healed. (Isaiah 53:4–5)

  Note: The last part of this verse ("by His stripes we are healed") clearly shows that your healing was paid for at the cross!
- "No weapon formed against you shall prosper, and every tongue which rises against you in judgment you shall condemn. This is the

heritage [birthright] of the servants of the LORD, and their righteousness is from Me," says the LORD. (Isaiah 54:17)

Note: Sickness is judging you falsely; it is your birthright to live in health. Condemn sickness with the Word of God, and command it to leave your body.

- Then your light shall break forth like the morning, your healing shall spring forth speedily, and your righteousness shall go before you; the glory of the LORD shall be your rear guard. (Isaiah 58:8)
- Heal me, O LORD, and I shall be healed; save me, and I shall be saved, for You are my praise. (Jeremiah 17:14)

  Note: Once a person finally sees that healing is a finished work along with salvation, paid for at the same time with the same healing blood of Christ, then you can get excited about this verse and say, "You did it, Lord, for me! Then according to this verse I will agree. I will have healing just as I have salvation!"
- "For I will restore health to you and heal you

of your wounds," says the LORD, "Because they called you an outcast saying: 'This is Zion; no one seeks her.'" (Jeremiah 30:17)

- Behold, I will bring it health and healing; I will heal them and reveal to them the abundance of peace and truth. (Jeremiah 33:6)
- In this manner, therefore, pray: Our Father in heaven, hallowed be Your name. Your kingdom come. Your will be done on earth as it is in heaven. (Matthew 6:9–10)

  Note: Jesus always prays the will of God, and He prays that the will of God be done here on the earth just as it is in heaven. People in heaven are not sick; so we can clearly see it is God's will that we also be free from sickness.
- Assuredly, I say to you, whatever you bind on earth will be bound in heaven, and whatever you loose on earth will be loosed in heaven. (Matthew 18:18)

  Note: The word *bind* means to forbid; the word *loose* means to let go or to allow to go free. Do not allow sickness, pain, or disease to run free in your body; bind it (forbid it) to stay there any longer. Put your foot down and command it to leave in the Name of Jesus!

- Again I say to you that if two of you agree on earth concerning anything that they ask, it will be done for them by My Father in heaven. (Matthew 18:19)

  Note: The prayer of agreement is powerful—have someone agree with you for your healing!

- Therefore I say to you, whatever things you ask when you pray, believe that you receive them, and you will have them. (Mark 11:24)
- And these signs will follow those who believe: In My name they will cast out demons; they will speak with new tongues; they will take up serpents; and if they drink anything deadly, it will by no means hurt them; they will lay hands on the sick, and they will recover. (Mark 16:17–18)

  Note: Find someone who believes God's Word regarding healing and have them lay hands on you and pray for you. (James 5:16 says that "the effective, fervent prayer of a righteous man avails much.")

- Behold, I give you the authority to trample on serpents and scorpions, and over all the power of the enemy, and nothing shall by any means hurt you. (Luke 10:19)

  Note: This is an exciting verse, as Jesus said He has given us authoritative power over *all* (not "some") of the enemy! Command Satan to take his hands off you. Command sickness and disease to leave you now in the name of Jesus.
- The thief [Satan] does not come except to steal, and to kill, and to destroy. I [Jesus] have come that they may have life, and that they may have it more abundantly. (John 10:10)

  Note: Here we see the desired will of the Lord for every believer—that we experience abundant life. According to this verse, He came for this very purpose. We also see clearly here that it is not God who afflicts us. The word here for life is the Greek word *zoe.* One commentator says that this word describes "the highest and best of which Christ is." You can easily see the wonderful gift of life the Lord wants for each of us. Sickness and disease are truly not in His plan for us, simply because He has no sickness of His own to give us.

- But if the Spirit of Him who raised Jesus from the dead dwells in you, He who raised Christ from the dead will also give life to your mortal [natural, earthly] bodies through His Spirit who dwells in you. (Romans 8:11)

  Note: Take a close look at this Scripture. This is talking about your body that you have now, not the one you're going to receive one day in heaven. Allow the Lord to impart His life into you now by placing faith in His Word. Begin to praise Him for this promise.

- What then shall we say to these things? If God is for us, who can be against us? (Romans 8:31)

  Note: You are a winner, you are victorious through the Lord Jesus Christ. Begin to see yourself the way God sees you.

- He who did not spare His own Son, but delivered Him up for us all, how shall He not with Him also freely give us all things? (Romans 8:32)

Note: Surely this includes healing!

- But we have this treasure in earthen vessels.... We are hard-pressed on every side...always carrying about in the body the dying of the Lord Jesus [which was for our victory], that the life of Jesus also may be manifested in our body. For we who live are always delivered to death for Jesus' sake, that the life of Jesus also may be manifested in our mortal flesh. (2 Corinthians 4:7–11)
- Now may the God of peace Himself sanctify you completely; and may your whole spirit, soul, and body be preserved blameless at the coming of our Lord Jesus Christ. (1 Thessalonians 5:23)

  Note: It is very clear in this passage that wholeness, wellness, and health are for the complete makeup of man—spiritual, mental, and physical.
- Is anyone among you sick? Let him call for the elders of the church, and let them pray over him, anointing him with oil in the name of the Lord. And the prayer of faith will save the sick, and the Lord will raise

him up. And if he has committed sins, he will be forgiven. (James 5:14–15)

- [Jesus]Himself bore our sins in His own body on the tree, that we, having died to sins, might live for righteousness—by whose stripes you were healed. (1 Peter 2:24)

  Note: This is past tense: "You were healed." Jesus paid it all for your total deliverance—spirit, soul, and body!

- His divine power has given to us all things that pertain to life and godliness, through the knowledge of Him who called us by glory and virtue, by which have been given to us exceedingly great and precious promises, that through these you may be partakers of the divine nature, having escaped the corruption that is in the world through lust. (2 Peter 1:3–4)

  Note: Notice the past tense—He"has" given us all things that pertain to life! The blessing of health was purchased for us at the cross; it belongs to you now. Notice the importance of the Word of God; your healing must be rooted steadfastly on the Word, not on what you see or how you feel.

- You are of God, little children, and have overcome them, because He who is in you is greater than he who is in the world. (1 John 4:4)
- For whatever is born of God overcomes the world. And this is the victory that has overcome the world—our faith. (1 John 5:4)

  Note: As a believer, we are given the right to overcome that which comes against us. We do not deny that the problem or circumstance exists; we do, however, deny that the problem has the right to stay! Faith in God is victory all of the time!
- Beloved, I pray that you may prosper in all things and be in health, just as your soul prospers. (3 John 1:2)

In Reverence and Worship

Make Jesus the Lord of your life; reverence Him by closing all doors to the enemy, giving first place to Jesus alone!

- Do not be wise in your own eyes; fear the Lord and depart from evil. It will be health to your flesh, and strength to your bones. (Proverbs 3:7–8)

Note: The term "fear the Lord" means to reverence and worship the Lord in all things.

- If you diligently heed the voice of the LORD your God and do what is right in His sight, give ear to His commandments and keep all His statutes, I will put [permit] none of the diseases on you which I have brought on the Egyptians. For I am the LORD who heals you. (Exodus 15:26)
- So you shall serve [worship] the LORD your God, and He will bless your bread and your water. And I will take sickness away from the midst of you. (Exodus 23:25)

  Note: True worship from the heart is a key to walking in divine health. Close every door you can to the devil.
- Because you have made the LORD, who is my refuge, even the Most High, your dwelling place, no evil shall befall you, nor shall any plague come near your dwelling. (Psalm 91:9–10)
- "But to you who fear [reverence, worship] My name the Sun of Righteousness shall arise with healing in His wings; and you

shall go out and grow fat like stall-fed calves. You shall trample the wicked, for they shall be ashes under the soles of your feet on the day that I do this," says the LORD of hosts. (Malachi 4:2–3)

Note: I love this verse! This verse is a great promise and even tells us when it became a reality for us: "On the day that I do this" was the day of Christ's death on Calvary. Now the enemy is "ashes" under our feet, and healing and protection belong to us. (See Luke 10:19 also.)

Healing Is the Lord's Will

Know that when you ask the Lord for healing, this is already His essential will for us, and He hears you and He agrees. Know that He has already settled it in the atonement through the blood of Jesus Christ—He says yes!

- O LORD my God, I cried out to You, and You healed me. (Psalm 30:2)
- Then they cried out to the LORD in their trouble, and He saved them out of their distresses. He sent His word and healed them, and delivered them from their destructions. (Psalm 107:19–20)

- Ask, and it will be given to you; seek, and you will find; knock, and it will be opened to you. For everyone who asks receives, and he who seeks finds, and to him who knocks it will be opened. (Matthew 7:7–8)

  Note: The word "ask" in the Greek has the meaning of insistent asking, with a knowledge of what belongs to the one making the request. It means presenting a solid requisition to God, knowing that He longs to distribute what He has to the one in need. (Look at James 1:5–8; we must ask in faith. And faith always knows; it never wishes!)

- Now this is the confidence that we have in Him, that if we ask anything according to His will, He hears us. And if we know that He hears us, whatever we ask, we know that we have the petitions that we have asked of Him. (1 John 5:14–15)

  Note: The Word of God is the will of God. If you see it in the Word of God, you can be assured that it is the will of God. The Lord is not trying to keep healing from you; He is trying to get it *to* you.

- For all the promises of God in Him are Yes, and in Him Amen, to the glory of God through us. (2 Corinthians 1:20)

    Note: Notice that all of God's promises toward us are "yes" and "amen" (meaning "So be it!" or "It is settled!"). There are no "no's" from the Lord to us when it comes to performing His Word.

THE WORD OF GOD BRINGS HEALING

- This is my comfort in my affliction, for Your word has given me life. (Psalm 119:50)
- So then faith comes by hearing, and hearing by the word of God. (Romans 10:17)

    Note: Faith for healing comes by hearing God's Word concerning healing. So just as you may be taking medicine two or three times a day, do the same thing with the promises in the Word of God regarding healing, and allow your faith to be built up! You'll be amazed at the change that will take place.

- My son, give attention to my words; incline your ear to my sayings. Do not let them depart from your eyes; keep them in the midst of your heart; for they are life to those who find them, and health [literally "medicine"] to all their flesh. (Proverbs 4:20–22)

Note: Here it is as plain as it can be: The taking of God's Word is life and medicine to your flesh. So just don't take the medicine your doctor prescribed; add the Word of God along with it. Prescribed medicine can heal and help some things, but God's medicine can heal all.

- And you shall know the truth, and the truth shall make you free. (John 8:32)

  Note: The Word of God is truth (see John 17:17). Once you know the truth concerning healing in God's redemptive plan, you can begin to exercise faith and expect the promises of God to be manifested in you. And they will be—REJOICE!

- All Scripture is given by inspiration of God, and is profitable for doctrine, for reproof, for correction, for instruction in righteousness, that the man of God may be complete, thoroughly equipped for every good work. (2 Timothy 3:16–17)

Note: Does your body or your mind need correction? God's Word is just the medicine, that you may be complete and thoroughly equipped for every good work. If you are sick you may be unable to do the work of the ministry; God wants you to be a living example in every area of His grace and mercy and power.

- It is the Spirit who gives life; the flesh profits nothing. The words that I speak to you are spirit, and they are life. (John 6:63)

  Note: God's Word is healing; it will bring health to your flesh (see Proverbs 4:22). That's why it's important to continue going over the healing Scriptures daily, building your faith in the area of healing, imparting the very life of God into your cells. Fill up on God's Word!

- If you abide in Me, and My words abide in you, you will ask what you desire, and it shall be done for you. (John 15:7)
- So shall My word be that goes forth from My mouth; it shall not return to Me void, but it shall accomplish what I please, and it

shall prosper in the thing for which I sent it. (Isaiah 55:11)

Note: God's Word on healing will accomplish healing in you.

- Then the LORD said to me, "You have seen well, for I am ready to perform My word." (Jeremiah 1:12)

  Note: God is looking, searching eagerly, for someone to take Him at His Word so He can perform it on their behalf.

- Not a word failed of any good thing which the LORD had spoken to the house of Israel. All came to pass. (Joshua 21:45)

  Note: How much more sure is this Old Covenant promise to us, since our New Covenant with God is based upon the shed blood of Jesus Christ!

Healing Is a Good Gift from God

- Every good gift and every perfect gift is from above, and comes down from the Father of lights, with whom there is no variation or shadow of turning. (James 1:17)

  Note: Healing is a wonderful gift from God, and here again is another proof that He does not change. What He did yesterday He will do again today. Praise the Lord, He is still the Healer!

- Therefore let no one boast in men. For all things are yours: whether Paul or Apollos or Cephas, or the world or life or death, or things present or things to come—all are yours. (1 Corinthians 3:21–22)

  Note: This says it so clearly: The Lord is holding nothing back from us. Surely healing is included in the claim of "all things," and certainly is included in the word "life." Begin to praise the Lord for your healing, which is a gift to you from the Lord, and for the manifestation that will come as you receive the promise by faith.

- For the gifts and the calling of God are irrevocable. (Romans 11:29)

  Note: He's the *Giver* of gifts and He doesn't take them back; they cannot be canceled out!

- For it is God who works in you both to will and to do for His good pleasure. (Philippians 2:13)

Redeemed from Bondage to Sickness and Disease

- Christ has redeemed us from the curse of the law, having become a curse for us (for it is written, "Cursed is everyone who hangs on a tree"), that the blessing of Abraham might come upon the Gentiles in Christ Jesus, that we might receive the promise of the Spirit through faith. (Galatians 3:13–14)

  Note: The curse of the law includes sickness and disease, and is found in Deuteronomy 28:15–68. (The first part of that chapter pertains to the blessing, and the rest of the chapter describes the curse.) By the shed blood of Jesus Christ we were purchased out of, or out from under, the curse!
- For the law of the Spirit of life in Christ Jesus has made me free from the law of sin and death. (Romans 8:2)
- He has delivered us from the power of darkness and conveyed us into the kingdom of the Son of His love. (Colossians 1:13)

  Note: Remember there is no sickness or disease in the kingdom of God! Here again is another wonderful Scripture proving your birthright of healing.

Rejoice in God's Promises

Snap out of that depression! Remember that your attitude determines your altitude!

- Therefore strengthen the hands which hang down, and the feeble knees, and make straight paths for your feet, so that what is lame may not be dislocated, but rather be healed. (Hebrews 12:12–13)

  Note: Real faith rejoices at the promises of God as if it were experiencing them already. Get your focus off of your problem and onto the answer, which is the promises of God—His Word. REJOICE! Get happy, it's all yours!

Your Source of Confidence

We can have confidence in Him, for God cannot lie!

- Let us hold fast the confession of our hope without wavering, for He who promised is faithful. (Hebrews 10:23)

  Note: Remember that Hebrews 6:18 tells us it is impossible for God to lie!

- Now this is the confidence that we have in Him, that if we ask anything according to His will, He hears us. And if we know that He hears us, whatever we ask, we know that we have the petitions that we have asked of Him. (1 John 5:14–15)

  Note: It's easy to know the will of God; the Word of God is the will of God! Jeremiah 1:12 says that He watches over His Word to perform it. So when you ask and believe the Word of God, you are asking and believing according to His will, and you will receive just as it says!

- Therefore do not cast away your confidence, which has great reward. For you have need of endurance, so that after you have done the will of God, you may receive the promise. (Hebrews 10:35–36)

  Note: Remember again that the will of God is the Word of God!

The Gift of Long Life

Long life belongs to you—don't give up! Base your faith on the promises of God.

- The days of our lives are seventy years; and if by reason of strength they are eighty years, yet their boast is only labor and sorrow; for it is soon cut off, and we fly away. (Psalm 90:10)

    Note: Did you see it! The essential plan of God is that we live at least a minimum of seventy years. Speak to that mountain of death and command it to be removed. Begin to grab hold of this promise and lay claim to it and say it with your mouth. Don't settle for less than what God has promised; don't let the devil steal from you—go on and live a long life fulfilling your days and ministry on this earth!

- You shall come to the grave at a full age, as a sheaf of grain ripens in its season. (Job 5:26)
- With long life I will satisfy him, and show him My salvation. (Psalms 91:16)
- I shall not die, but live, and declare the works of the LORD. (Psalm 118:17)

    Note: Agree with this right now! Declare it with your voice! God has a plan for your life here on the earth. Don't let the enemy steal it away. You can do what God says you can do; you can be what God says you can be!

Every Thought Captive

Cast down those thoughts and imaginations that don't line up with the Word of God!

- Bringing every thought into captivity to the obedience of Christ. (2 Corinthians 10:4–5)

  Note: Keep your focus on the promises of God. Make yourself stay focused. Don't allow your mind to stray—the manifestation of your healing is on its way!

State Your Case to God!

- I, even I, am He who blots out your transgressions for My own sake; and I will not remember your sins. Put Me in remembrance; let us contend together; state your case, that you may be acquitted. (Isaiah 43:25–26)

  Note: Your case was settled when Jesus went to the cross on your behalf! If you have accepted Jesus Christ as Lord, then "it is finished"!

Your Words Are Important

- "I create the fruit of the lips: Peace, peace to him who is far off and to him who is near," says the LORD, "and I will heal him." (Isaiah 57:19)

  Note: The word *fruit* here means what is "produced." God creates what you produce from your mouth when we believe and speak the Word of God.

- Have faith in God. For assuredly, I say to you, whoever says to this mountain, "Be removed and be cast into the sea," and does not doubt in his heart, but believes that those things he says will be done, he will have whatever he says. (Mark 11:22–23)

  Note: What kind of mountains or obstacles do you have in your life right now? Obey Jesus and command that mountain of pain, cancer, or disease to go out of your body now, in the name of Jesus. Begin to call your body whole, healed, well. Don't stop; don't listen to your body; listen to Jesus!

Give Testimony of Your Healing

- And they overcame him by the blood of the Lamb and by the word of their testimony, and they did not love their lives to the death. (Revelation 12:11)

  Note: When your healing manifests itself and you recover and have the opportunity to testify to the grace of the Lord—do it! The Lord wants you to give glory to Him for what He has done, and it will also serve to help build faith in someone else who has a need.

Your Journal

Write down your answer to this question: How can your own life change as you take the Lord at His word, and claim His healing?

ACKNOWLEDGEMENTS

How wonderful it is to have someone in your corner all the time! My wonderful husband of over forty-four years, George Wells, continually encourages me by telling me, "You can do it, baby."

My son is one of my best Hollywood agents because he tells people how proud he is of his mother and that there's not much she cannot do well. (He's biased.) He tells me, "Mama, you're my hero. You know how to do everything well. You are an "I Can" woman."

My daughters are my confidantes and prayer partners. They believe, without a doubt, that in Christ we can be our best because God has given us the authority to do His will.

My literary agent, David Van Diest, suggested the title of this book, and I've been excited about it ever since. It's marvelous to have an agent who's as concerned about the spiritual tenet and biblical content of this book as he is with the book deal itself. Thank you, David.

Most of all, I want to thank God for revealing to us who He is and what He can mean in everyone's life. He, indeed, is the Great I AM.

Thanks to the publisher, Multnomah, for seeing the value of a book like this. It is my sincere desire that when people read this book, they will be strengthened by its content, renewed by its encouragement, restored by its life lessons, reconciled by its deliverance power, and regenerated by its heartfelt sincerity.

Holy Father, thank You for teaching me that I CAN... BECAUSE I KNOW THE I AM.

....

The author's recording "His Glorious Grace:
Testimony in Song"
is available from:

A Woman of God Ministries
1934 Lanark Avenue
Dallas, Texas 75203

1-800-843-5622

www.thelmawells.com